How to Play Tennis for Beginners

The Ultimate Guide to Mastering Everything from Rules, Tennis Racket, and Etiquette to Serve, Scoring, and Tips for Single and Doubles

Table of Contents

Introduction

This guide introduces newcomers to the exhilarating world of tennis, a sport marked by its strategic complexity, physical demands, and rich history. Whether you're picking up a racket for the first time or looking to solidify your understanding of the sport's fundamentals, this guide is tailored to provide a comprehensive journey through every aspect of the game.

The initial chapters delve into the basics of tennis, from understanding the rules and scoring system to choosing the right equipment. The importance of tennis etiquette, often an overlooked aspect of the game, is highlighted, setting the stage for a respectful and enjoyable experience on the court.

From there, the guide transitions into the physical aspects of the game, breaking down every fundamental technique, from the serve to the volley, forehand, backhand, and beyond. Detailed explanations, strategies, and tips are provided to help beginners develop a well-rounded game.

More advanced aspects of tennis, such as strategic play in singles and doubles games, are also covered. The guide explores the importance of physical fitness and mental fortitude, both essential aspects for any player looking to excel in this sport.

Finally, several advanced practice drills are introduced to push players beyond their comfort zones and take their game to the next level.

The journey ahead is filled with fascinating insights, practical instructions, and a depth of knowledge aiming to inspire, instruct, and ignite a passion for this popular game. Remember, every grand slam champion, every weekend warrior, and every enthusiastic amateur started as a beginner. With patience, practice, and persistence, the journey from beginner to skilled player can be an incredibly rewarding experience.

Chapter 1: Understanding the Game of Tennis

Tennis, a globally recognized sport, combines physical prowess, strategic gameplay, and mental toughness. Originating from a handball-like game played by ancient cultures, it has evolved into a sport enjoyed by millions. Played on a variety of surfaces, from grass to clay to hard courts, the game of tennis can be a leisurely pastime or a fiercely competitive professional sport.

Tennis is a sport that transcends borders and cultures. Its universal appeal is evident in its global fan base, with major tournaments, such as the Grand Slam events—Wimbledon, the Australian Open, the French Open, and the US Open—drawing millions of spectators from around the world. The sport is played at various levels, from amateur community leagues to high-stakes professional circuits, and is a highlight of the Olympic Games.

The popularity of tennis is attributable not only to the thrill and challenge of gameplay but also to the personal development it fosters. The sport cultivates discipline, resilience, quick thinking, and physical fitness, making it a holistic approach to personal growth.

This chapter delves into the fascinating world of tennis, tracing its roots and evolution, understanding its rules and scoring system, and appreciating its place in the world today. Whether a seasoned fan, a recreational player, or a curious newcomer to the sport, this guide aims to provide a comprehensive understanding of this captivating game.

The Origins and Evolution of Tennis

The Birth of Tennis

Tennis origins can be traced back to the 12th century in northern France, where it emerged as a game called "jeu de paume" (game of the palm). In this early version, players used their hand, or a glove, instead of a racket to strike a ball over a net or against a wall. Courts were typically in enclosed areas, like courtyards or monasteries, and the game quickly gained popularity among the clergy and the nobility.

The sport evolved, with rackets appearing in the game around the 16th century. These early rackets were made of wood and strung with sheep gut, a far cry from the sophisticated equipment in today's game. The first known instances of a game resembling modern tennis can be attributed to Major Walter Clopton Wingfield, who, in 1873, patented a game he called "Sphairistikè" (Greek for "the art of playing ball"). He established the hourglass-shaped court, the net, the scoring method, and the basic rules forming the foundation of modern tennis.

In 1877, the All-England Croquet Club held its first lawn tennis tournament to raise funds. This event, now known as Wimbledon, is the oldest tennis tournament in the world and one of the four Grand Slam events. It was instrumental in standardizing the game's rules and court dimensions.

From these humble beginnings, tennis spread across Europe and eventually to the United States, where it was played in clubs and private courts before becoming the widespread public sport it is today. The game's evolution was marked by the formation of official governing bodies, such as the International Lawn Tennis Federation in 1913, now known as the International Tennis Federation.

The birth of tennis is a rich narrative marked by continual evolution and growth. From its origins as a handball game among French nobility to the high-speed, strategic sport of today, tennis' history is as dynamic and engaging as the game itself.

The Evolution of Tennis

Tennis, like many other sports, has evolved significantly since its inception. Changes and improvements in equipment, rules, and playing style have characterized this evolution.

1. Changes and Improvements in Equipment

The most striking changes have occurred in the equipment. Early tennis rackets were simple wooden frames with tight strings made from sheep gut. However, the 20th century saw a shift to lighter, more durable materials. By the 1980s, manufacturers used graphite, a light yet strong material, allowing the production of larger, more powerful rackets.

Balls have also changed over time. Originally made of leather filled with wool or hair, today's tennis balls are made of rubber and covered with felt. This change made the balls more durable and easier to see during play.

2. Changes in Rules

The rules of tennis have also evolved over the years. The tiebreak rule, introduced in the 1970s, is a prime example. Before its introduction, matches could potentially go on indefinitely. The tiebreak system was proposed to ensure games were more time-efficient and exciting for spectators.

Similarly, the Hawk-Eye system was introduced as a mechanism to challenge referee calls in 2002. This computer system generates a 3D representation of the ball's trajectory and has brought a new level of accuracy to decision-making in the game.

3. The Transition from "Real Tennis" to Modern Tennis

The transition from "real tennis" or "royal tennis" to the modern game was marked by several significant changes. Real tennis was played indoors, with complex rules reflecting the game's courtly origins. The move to the outdoors simplified the game, making it more accessible to the general public.

The modern game also standardized the court size and shape, moving away from the hourglass shape proposed by Major Walter Clopton Wingfield to the rectangular court of today. This change allowed for more uniform gameplay and made competitions fairer.

The evolution of tennis is a testament to the sport's adaptability and enduring appeal. Through changes in equipment, rules, and playing style, tennis has become a faster, more exciting, and more accessible sport. It has retained its classic charm while evolving to meet the demands of a changing world.

Significant Milestones

Tennis history is marked by significant milestones that have shaped the game. Some of these milestones include the advent of professional tennis and the introduction of the Grand Slam tournaments.

1. Major Events in Tennis History

One of the most important events in tennis history was the first Wimbledon Championship, held in 1877. It was the first tennis tournament to gain international recognition, and its rules largely shaped the modern game of tennis.

The Davis Cup, established in 1900, is another significant event. Initially a match between the United States and Great Britain, the Davis Cup grew to become one of the most prestigious team events in men's tennis.

The establishment of the International Tennis Federation (ITF) in 1913 was another key event. The ITF was crucial in standardizing the rules of the game and organizing international competitions.

2. The Start of Professional Tennis

The beginning of the professional era in tennis in 1968, known as the "Open Era," marked a significant shift in the sport. Before this, only amateur players were allowed to compete in major tournaments. The Open Era meant that professional players could compete in all tournaments, leading to a rise in the competitiveness and quality of tennis. This era also paved the way for players to make a living from the sport, attracting more talent and raising the playing standards.

3. The Advent of Grand Slam Tournaments

The introduction of the Grand Slam tournaments has been crucial to the popularity and prestige of tennis. The four Grand Slam tournaments—Wimbledon, the Australian Open, the French Open, and the US Open—are the most important events in professional tennis. Winning a Grand Slam title is considered the highest achievement in the sport.

Each tournament is unique, played on different surfaces and conditions, providing varied challenges for the players. They also offer the most ranking points, prize money, and public and media attention, making them highly sought-after titles.

Over time, these tournaments have produced some of the sport's greatest moments and champions, contributing significantly to tennis' popularity and global reach.

These significant milestones have shaped tennis, helping it transition from a game for the elite to a global sport enjoyed by millions. They have contributed to the sports' professionalization, increasing its competitiveness and stature in the sports world.

The Modern Game

Moving on to the present day, the state of tennis continues to evolve. Today, the sport is characterized by intense global competition, the rise of technology, and the dominance of certain players and nations.

1. The State of Tennis Today

Tennis today is a global sport enjoyed by millions of people around the world. It's played at various levels, from local community leagues to high-stakes professional tournaments. The sport continues to grow, with increasing participation rates and viewer numbers.

Professional tennis, in particular, is characterized by high competition. The physicality, skill, and mental toughness required have never been greater. This intensity has resulted in some of the most exciting and memorable matches in the sport's history.

2. Top Players and Dominant Nations

Over the years, various players and nations have dominated the sport. Players like Novak Djokovic, Rafael Nadal, and Roger Federer have significantly impacted men's tennis. Serena Williams, Naomi Osaka, and Ashleigh Barty have substantially influenced women's tennis.

Nations like the United States, Spain, Switzerland, and Australia have traditionally been strong in tennis, producing multiple Grand Slam winners. However, the sport continues to spread, and new talent is emerging from countries not traditionally known for tennis.

3. The Rise of Technology and Its Impact on Tennis

Technology has had a profound impact on modern tennis. Racket and string technology has evolved, allowing players to hit harder, more accurate shots. Technology has improved fitness and training methods, allowing players to reach higher physical conditioning.

Perhaps most notably, the introduction of electronic line-calling systems, like Hawk-Eye, has brought a new precision to the game. These systems use multiple cameras and complex algorithms to track the ball's trajectory and determine whether a shot was in or out. This technology has reduced human error in officiating and added an exciting element to the sport for spectators.

The modern game of tennis is a dynamic, global sport characterized by intense competition, the dominance of exceptional players and nations, and the integration of advanced technology. It continues to captivate audiences worldwide, uniting people through a shared love for this exciting and challenging game.

The Basic Rules and Scoring System

The Tennis Court

A standard tennis court is a flat, rectangular surface measuring 78 feet (23.77 meters) in length and 27 feet (8.23 meters) in width for singles matches. For doubles matches, the width extends to 36 feet (10.97 meters) to include the doubles alleys on each side.

The court is divided in half by a net standing 3.5 feet (1.07 meters) high at the posts and 3 feet (0.914 meters) high in nter. The court is marked with various lines defining undaries and serving specific purposes. These include:

- **Baseline**: This is the line at the end of each side of the court. Players usually serve from behind this line.

- **Service Boxes:** The service line divides the court into two service boxes on each side. The service boxes are where the ball must land when a player serves.

- **Center Mark:** A small mark in the center of the baseline is used to determine the serving side.

- **Singles Sideline**: The sideline for singles play.

- **Doubles Sideline:** The wider sideline for doubles play.

Player Equipment

- **Racket:** The tennis racket consists of a handled frame with a wide-open hoop and a stretched network of strings. It is used to strike the tennis ball.

- **Ball:** The tennis ball is typically yellow and made of hollow rubber with a felt covering. Its diameter ranges from 2.57 to 2.70 inches (65.41 to 68.58 mm).

- **Attire:** Players typically wear comfortable, breathable clothing suitable for physical activity. Most players also wear tennis shoes designed to provide the right grip for the court surface.

Basic Rules

- **Serving:** Each point begins with a serve initiated from behind the baseline. The server must alternate between the right and left sides of the court (as determined by the center mark) with each new point. The serve must land in the diagonally opposite service box.

- **Scoring:** Points are scored as 15 (for the first point), 30 (second), and 40 (third). If the score is tied at 40-40, this is referred to as 'deuce.' If a game reaches 'deuce,' a player must win by two points.

- **Faults:** If the server misses the service box on the first serve, it's called a fault, and they get a second chance to serve. If the second serve also misses, it's called a double fault, and the other player wins the point.

- **In and Out Calls:** If a ball hits on or within the court's boundary lines, it's considered 'in.' If it hits outside the boundary lines, it's 'out'.

- **Umpire and Line Judges:** The chair umpire oversees the match, while line judges monitor the lines to determine whether shots are in or out. In professional tennis, disputed calls can be reviewed using electronic line-calling technology like Hawk-Eye.

The Scoring System

- **Points, Games, Sets, and Matches:** The player who scores four points wins a game, provided they are at least two points ahead. The player who wins six games wins a set, provided they are at least two games ahead. A tiebreak game is played if the set score reaches 6-6. The player who wins two sets (in most matches) or three sets (in men's singles at Grand Slams and Davis Cup) wins the match.

- **Tiebreak Rules**: In a tiebreak, players continue to serve and return, but the scoring is different (1, 2, 3, etc.). The first player to reach seven points and are at least two points ahead wins the tiebreak and the set.

- **Advantage**: In games that reach 'deuce,' the first point won gives that player the 'advantage.' If the player with the advantage wins the next point, they win the game. If they lose the next point, the score returns to 'deuce'.

While the rules of tennis can seem complex to a newcomer, with a little practice, they quickly become second nature. The game's unique scoring system adds an extra layer of strategy and excitement to the sport.

Chapter 2: Essential Tennis Gear

Embarking on a tennis journey can be an exciting adventure, but the array of equipment options can appear overwhelming for a newcomer. This chapter offers an in-depth guide for beginners to navigate this essential process of selecting the right tennis gear.

The chapter begins by exploring the importance of choosing a suitable tennis racket. Factors such as size, weight, grip, and materials will be examined to provide a comprehensive understanding. Following this, the focus shifts to tennis shoes, explaining their crucial role in performance and safety on the court.

The journey continues with a detailed look at tennis balls, an often overlooked yet vital component of the game. The different types available and how the correct choice can significantly impact play will be discussed. Lastly, the chapter covers other indispensable tennis accessories, including the appropriate tennis bag, comfortable and functional apparel, and important considerations for hydration and nutrition.

The chapter aims to provide knowledge for making informed decisions about tennis equipment. It endeavors to enhance the comfort, safety, and overall performance of new tennis players while increasing their enjoyment of the game.

Selecting the Right Tennis Racket

2. Your tennis racket should be tailored to your needs. Source: https://unsplash.com/photos/8E1Yplw6Hho?utm_source=unsplash&utm_medium=referral&utm_content=creditShareLink

Tailoring the tennis racket to a beginner's needs is integral to developing proper technique and form. Several key factors must be considered when choosing a starter racket.

The racket's parts determine its characteristics. The handle provides grip and stability, while the frame confers stability and power transfer. The string bed is the actual hitting surface. Different shapes and sizes affect how the racket performs.

Racket size impacts play significantly. Longer rackets provide more reach but less control. Larger head sizes are typically easier to use but less accurate. For beginners, shorter and smaller-headed rackets are often recommended.

Racket weight trades power for control. Heavier rackets generate more power but require more energy to swing. Lighter rackets allow quicker swings and shot repeats but lack punch. Beginners typically benefit from lighter rackets to facilitate further technique development.

Grip size should allow all fingers to fit comfortably while still providing security. An ill-fitted grip leads to unwanted movements during impact and imprecise shots.

Different materials are used in racket production, each changing the racket's weight, power, and feel. Graphite is lightweight and powerful, while materials like aluminum provide more control at the cost of weight. More forgiving materials best serve beginners.

Choosing Appropriate Tennis Shoes

The selection of appropriate tennis shoes is a critical element in the sport. The right footwear enhances performance and ensures safety and comfort during play. The importance of specific tennis shoes for the sport cannot be overstated, as they provide the necessary support and stability for the swift, lateral, and forward-backward movements unique to tennis.

A wide range of tennis shoe types are available on the market, each catering to specific needs, skill levels, and court surfaces. Some shoes are designed with an emphasis on stability, providing extra support to prevent ankle rolling.

Others focus on speed, featuring lightweight materials to allow quick and agile movements. Durability-focused shoes are built to withstand the rigorous demands of the sport and offer a longer lifespan, especially for players who often play on hard courts. Understanding these types and their unique features is crucial when selecting tennis shoes.

3. Tennis shoes should provide support for the necessary positions and movements needed throughout the game. Source: Jjanhone, CC BY-SA 4.0 <https://creativecommons.org/licenses/by-sa/4.0>, via Wikimedia Commons: https://commons.wikimedia.org/wiki/File:Wilson_Rush_Pro_tenn is_shoes.jpg

Another essential factor to consider is finding the right size and fit for tennis shoes. Shoes that are too loose or too tight can cause discomfort, hamper performance, and lead to injuries over time. A well-fitting tennis shoe should offer a snug yet comfortable fit, providing ample support for the heel and arch and allowing for some wiggle room for the toes. It's recommended to try shoes on later in the day, as feet usually swell during the day. Also, always try them on with the same sock types that will be worn during play.

Lastly, the court surface is significant in shoe selection. Different court surfaces, such as clay, grass, and hard courts, have varying effects on how a player moves and how much wear and tear the shoes endure. For instance, clay courts require shoes with a full herringbone tread pattern to provide the best traction and prevent the clay from clogging the soles. On the other hand, grass courts demand shoes with nubs or pimples on the sole for better grip, as the surface can be slippery. Hard court surfaces are tough on shoes and require footwear balanced with durability, support, and cushioning to withstand the impact.

Choosing appropriate tennis shoes means understanding the importance of specific tennis footwear, getting to know the different types available, finding the right size and fit, and taking into account the court surface. Considering these factors, the selection process becomes more straightforward and ensures a better tennis experience.

Understanding Tennis Balls and Their Types

Tennis balls, often taken for granted, are a fundamental element of the sport. Their design and construction have evolved over years of research and development, resulting in today's standard tennis balls. The design of a tennis ball is a feat of engineering, balancing various factors to provide the perfect blend of speed, bounce, and durability.

4. Tennis balls are engineered to provide the perfect blend of speed, bounce, and durability. Source: https://unsplash.com/photos/K9HgyI3qmqA?utm_source=unsplash&utm_medium=referral&utm_content=creditShareLink

The standard tennis ball is spherical with a diameter of roughly 6.7 cm and is covered in a high-visibility, fluorescent yellow felt, tightly bound to the rubber shell. The felt cover is not merely aesthetic; it serves several important purposes. Firstly, it enhances visibility for players and spectators. Secondly, it adds drag, slowing the ball down and making it easier to hit. Lastly, the felt creates the friction necessary for players to apply spin to their shots, a critical aspect of advanced play.

Tennis balls can generally be categorized into two primary types, which are pressure-less and pressurized.

Pressurized tennis balls are perhaps the most common and used in professional matches. These balls have a hollow rubber core filled with air or nitrogen under pressure, giving them a high bounce and speed. They're known for their lively and responsive feel. However, the downside to pressurized balls is that they lose their bounce over time as the pressurized gas inside the ball slowly leaks out, decreasing performance.

On the other hand, pressureless tennis balls have a solid core, giving them a different feel when compared to their pressurized counterparts. They are less bouncy and slower initially, but unlike pressurized balls, their bounce characteristics improve as the outer felt cover wears down. Pressureless balls are more durable and maintain their bounce for longer, making them a popular choice for practice, recreational play, and ball machines.

For beginners, the choice of a tennis ball is a crucial decision. While pressurized balls offer a more professional feel and faster play, their lifespan is limited. Pressureless balls, while initially less lively, offer long-lasting bounce and could be a more cost-effective choice for beginners still learning and practicing the basics of the game. There are also stage-specific balls for beginners, like the red (stage 3), orange (stage 2), and green (stage 1) balls, which are lower in compression and bounce, making them easier to hit and control.

In essence, understanding the basics of tennis balls, the different types available, and their unique characteristics can significantly influence the choice of the ball. This understanding optimizes the learning process and overall playing experience, especially for beginners.

Other Essential Tennis Accessories

A complete tennis kit goes beyond the quintessential racket, shoes, and balls. Several other accessories can enhance the tennis experience, ensuring comfort, convenience, and safety during play.

A good tennis bag is an essential accessory for a tennis player. It is a convenient storage solution, keeping all tennis equipment organized and protected. Tennis bags come in various shapes and sizes, from backpacks to shoulder totes to multi-racket bags. When selecting a tennis bag, considerations should be made for the number of rackets it can hold, storage space for other equipment like balls, water bottles, towels, and extra apparel, and if it has separate compartments for dirty or wet gear. Also, the bag's material should be durable to withstand outdoor conditions.

Tennis apparel is significant for a player's comfort and performance on the court. Specialized tennis clothing provides optimum flexibility and freedom of movement, which is paramount during a tennis game. When selecting tennis apparel, consider the clothing material. Fabrics should be lightweight and breathable to allow efficient heat management and sweat-wicking. The clothing fit is also important. It should be well-fitted but not restrictive, allowing players to move freely and comfortably.

Tennis caps and visors are not merely fashion accessories; they serve a functional purpose on the tennis court. These accessories provide crucial protection against the sun and help reduce glare, which could influence visibility during play. Caps and visors also aid in keeping sweat off the face, ensuring a more comfortable playing experience.

Hydration and nutrition are vital aspects of any sport, and tennis is no exception. Having a water bottle on hand during play, particularly during long sessions or in hot weather, to prevent dehydration is important. Some tennis bags come equipped with insulated pockets to keep water cool. For lengthy matches, snacks like energy bars, bananas, or nuts can provide a quick energy source to maintain performance levels.

While not directly part of the game, these additional accessories are crucial for a player's overall tennis experience. Carefully considering these elements, from choosing a suitable tennis bag to selecting appropriate apparel, protective headgear, and attention to hydration and nutrition, can significantly enhance comfort, performance, and enjoyment on the tennis court.

Chapter 3: Mastering the Fundamentals

This chapter aims to establish the foundational knowledge required to play tennis effectively. It delves into the basic elements every tennis player, regardless of their level, must understand and master.

This chapter is your steppingstone into the dynamic world of tennis. Before diving into the specifics, a solid understanding of why mastering the basics is crucial in any sport, especially tennis, is important.

In tennis, the fundamentals form the backbone of your playing style. They are the first building block in developing your game and the foundation upon which all your future skills are built. Without a solid grasp of the fundamentals, you will struggle to execute more advanced techniques correctly.

This chapter covers the basic elements of tennis, including grip and hand positions, proper stance and footwork, basic shots like the forehand and backhand, and mastering the serve. Each section gives detailed explanations, supplemented with diagrams and photos, to clarify the concepts discussed.

Grip and Hand Positions

Understanding the different grips in tennis is crucial for developing a well-rounded game. The grip a player chooses can influence the shots they can execute, the power behind their shots, and control over the ball. This section discusses three of the most common tennis grips: the Eastern, Western, and Continental grips.

Eastern Grip

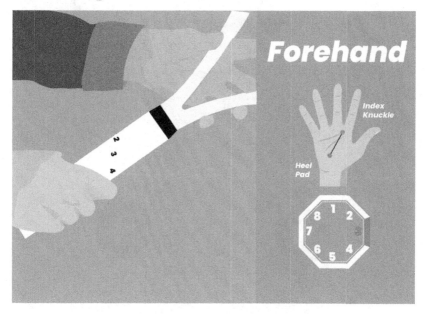

5.   *The Eastern grip. Source: https://images.squarespace-cdn.com/content/v1/5cfeebad9de45a0001980d17/1581625202540-WCPVJUV7XSJJPMM6OBGK/forehand-tennis-grip-indie-tenis.jpg*

The Eastern grip is one of the most traditional grips in tennis. The base knuckle of the index finger is placed on the third bevel of the tennis racket to form the Eastern grip. This grip is often used for forehand shots due to its natural feel and the ability to generate flat, powerful shots.

The advantages of the Eastern grip include its versatility and the ability to hit powerful shots with less effort. It also allows greater control over the direction of the ball. However, the Eastern grip might be challenging for high-bouncing balls, as it can be difficult to generate topspin.

Western Grip

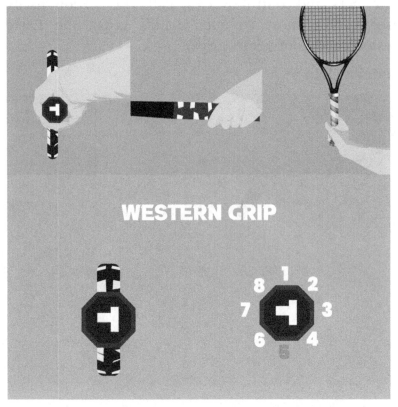

6. The Western Grip. Source:
https://sportsedtv.com/img/blog/forehand%20western%20grip.jp
g

The Western grip is where you place the base knuckle of the index finger on the fifth bevel of the tennis racket. This grip is popular among players who prefer a high-bouncing ball and favor topspin shots.

The Western grip offers a significant advantage with high-bouncing balls and provides excellent topspin. However, it can be harder to achieve flat shots or slices with this grip. Additionally, it can be more physically demanding due to the extreme wrist position required.

Continental Grip

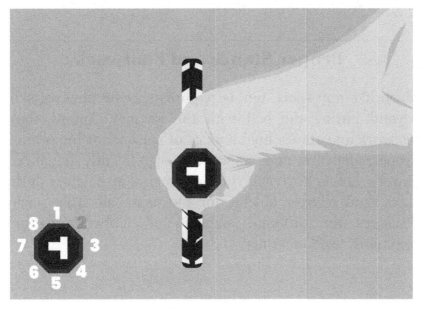

7. *The Continental grip. Source: https://tenniscompanion.org/wp-content/uploads/2020/03/continental-forehand-tennis-grip-view-from-behind-guide.png*

The Continental grip places the base knuckle of the index finger on the second bevel of the tennis racket. It is the most versatile grip, as it can be used for a variety of shots, including serves, volleys, overheads, and slices.

One major advantage of the Continental grip is its versatility, making it a good grip to master for all-around gameplay. However, the Continental grip may not provide as much power or topspin on groundstrokes as the Eastern or Western grips.

Understanding and mastering these different grips is core to mastering the fundamentals of tennis. Each grip has unique advantages and disadvantages and can significantly influence a player's style and performance on the court. Experiment with these different grips and understand which grip, or combination of grips, best suits your playing style and the situation on the court.

Proper Stance and Footwork

Much like any sport, tennis requires specific physical skills beyond hitting the ball with the racquet. Among these, footwork and stance hold a place of paramount importance. Proper footwork and stance can significantly enhance a player's ability to reach the ball, maintain balance during shots, and recover quickly for the next ball. This section discusses the different stances and footwork patterns commonly used in tennis.

Stances

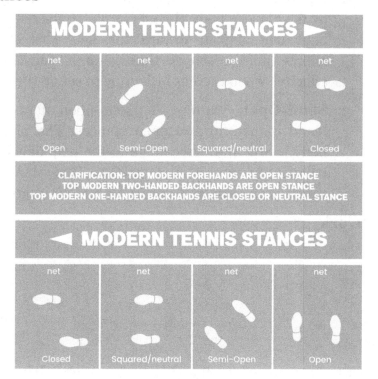

8. *Tennis stances. Source:*
https://images.prismic.io/coachtube/af7d49f1162fcf6bdf3
c14da706974cdc78d87c0_modern-tennis-
stances.jpg?auto=compress,format

Tennis stances refer to the positioning and alignment of a player's feet when preparing to hit the ball. Three primary stances in tennis are neutral, open, and semi-open stance.

1. **Neutral Stance**: In the neutral stance, the player's feet are roughly shoulder-width apart, with the foot on the same side as the hitting arm placed slightly forward. The player's body is generally perpendicular to the net. The neutral stance provides substantial balance and stability, making it suitable for powerful shots and precision.

2. **Open Stance:** The open stance is characterized by the player's body almost parallel to the net, with both feet aligned toward the net. This stance allows quick response times and is particularly effective when there is little time to set up the shot.

3. **Semi-Open Stance:** The semi-open stance is a blend of neutral and open stances. The player's body is at a 45-degree angle to the net, allowing a balance of power and agility. This stance is versatile and effective in various match situations.

Footwork

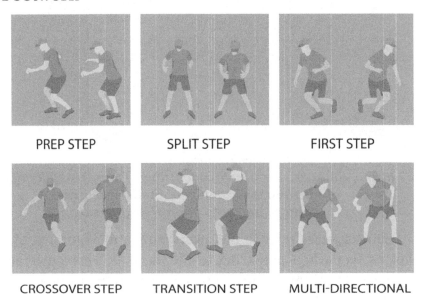

PREP STEP   SPLIT STEP   FIRST STEP

CROSSOVER STEP   TRANSITION STEP   MULTI-DIRECTIONAL

9. Tennis footwork drills. Source: https://kajabi-storefronts-production.kajabi-cdn.com/kajabi-storefronts-production/sites/28518/images/hLa9NcRoQgOOuo41vbUX_file.jpg

Footwork refers to the movement patterns players use to move around the court. Efficient footwork enables players to reach the ball quickly, maintain balance, and recover promptly.

1. **Shuffle Step:** The shuffle step is a basic footwork pattern where the player moves sideways by pushing off with the outer foot and dragging the inner foot to maintain balance. This movement is efficient for covering short distances quickly and is often used during volleys and baseline rallies.

2. **Crossover Step:** In the crossover step, the player crosses one foot over the other to move quickly in a particular direction. This footwork pattern is useful for rapidly covering larger distances, like when chasing down wide shots.

3. **Split Step:** The split step is a small, quick hop players make as their opponent strikes the ball. This movement helps prime the player's body for quick directional changes and is fundamental for reactive tennis footwork.

Good footwork and proper stance are integral to performing well in tennis. They enable players to move efficiently on the court, maintain balance during shots, and set up properly for each stroke. Understanding these different stances and footwork patterns is crucial for developing a strong foundation in tennis.

Basic Shots

In tennis, two core shots form the basis of every player's game and these are the forehand and the backhand. Mastering these shots is key to becoming a proficient player. This section delves into the intricacies of these fundamental shots, providing a comprehensive understanding of the techniques, forms, and appropriate situations to use them.

Forehand

10. *Forehand shot. Source: Nikko5555, CC BY-SA 3.0 <https://creativecommons.org/licenses/by-sa/3.0>, via Wikimedia Commons: https://commons.wikimedia.org/wiki/File:Nole_Forehand_3.jpg*

The forehand is typically the first shot learned in tennis and is often the most comfortable and powerful shot in a player's repertoire. The forehand shot is performed with the palm facing the ball.

1. **Grip:** The Eastern and Western grips are commonly used for the forehand shot. The grip a player chooses can significantly influence the forehand they execute. The Eastern grip is generally used for flatter shots, and the Western grip for shots with more topspin.

2. **Stance:** The stance used for the forehand shot can be open, semi-open, or neutral. The stance choice depends on the player's position on the court, the

height and speed of the incoming ball, and the player's individual style and comfort.

3. **Swing:** The forehand swing starts with the racquet's back and the non-dominant arm pointing toward the incoming ball. As the ball approaches, the racquet is swung forward to meet the ball, with the point of contact ideally slightly in front of the body and around waist height. The swing should be smooth and fluid, using the entire body, not only the arm.

4. **Follow-Through:** After making contact with the ball, the racquet should continue its path forward and upward, finishing high above the shoulder. This follow-through is vital for maintaining control over the shot and generating topspin.

Backhand

The backhand shot is performed with the back of the hand facing the ball. The backhand can be hit with one or two hands, with each method having advantages and nuances.

1. **Single-Handed Backhand**: The single-handed backhand is typically performed with an Eastern or Continental grip. The swing starts with the racquet's back and the non-dominant arm pointing toward the incoming ball. The point of contact should be slightly in front of the body and around waist height. The follow-through completes with the racquet finishing high, over the shoulder.

2. **Double-Handed Backhand:** The double-handed backhand provides more stability and control and is often easier for beginners to learn. The grip for the double-handed backhand is

typically an Eastern forehand grip with the dominant hand and a Continental grip with the non-dominant hand. The swing and follow-through are similar to the single-handed backhand, but with both hands on the racquet, providing more power and control.

11. Double-handed backhand. Source: Carine06, CC BY-SA 2.0 <https://creativecommons.org/licenses/by-sa/2.0>, via Wikimedia Commons: https://commons.wikimedia.org/wiki/File:Andy_Murray_Backha nd_(1).jpg

The forehand and backhand are the most fundamental shots in tennis. They form the basis of a player's groundstroke game and are essential for maintaining rallies and constructing points. Understanding the techniques and forms for these shots is a crucial step in mastering the basics of tennis.

Mastering the Serve

The serve is one of the most crucial shots in tennis. This shot initiates every point and can set the tone for the entire rally. Mastering the serve requires understanding and practice of various elements, such as the stance, grip, toss, swing, and follow-through.

Stance

The serving stance is typically a platform or pinpoint stance. In a platform stance, the feet are shoulder-width apart, parallel to the baseline, with the back foot remaining stationary throughout the serve. The pinpoint stance brings the back foot up to the front foot during the serve, leading to a more linear motion toward the net.

Grip

The most commonly used grip for serving is the Continental grip. This grip allows players to hit various serves, including flat, slice, and kick serve and provides the best combination of power, spin, and control.

Toss

The toss is a critical aspect of the serve. Ideally, the ball should be tossed high enough to allow full extension of the arm on the swing but not so high that it starts to drop significantly before contact. The ball should be tossed slightly into the court and to the right (for right-handed players) for a first serve and slightly to the left for a second serve to allow more spin.

Swing

The swing on a serve is a complex sequence of motions often called the "trophy pose." It involves bending the knees, tilting the torso back, and pulling the racquet back into a trophy-like position. From there, the player pushes up and forward with their legs, extending their hitting arm toward the ball and pronating their forearm to make contact with the ball.

Follow-Through

After contact, the racquet continues moving forward and down, finishing on the opposite side of the body. The player's momentum should carry them into the court, ready to respond to the return shot.

Types of Serves

12. The types of serves. Source:
https://i.ytimg.com/vi/RReBwUHe1ug/maxresdefault.jpg

The three main serve types are flat, slice, and kick.

1. **Flat Serve**: The flat serve is the most straightforward and typically the fastest. It involves hitting the ball with a direct, flat hit, offering less margin for error over the net and potentially a more powerful and difficult-to-return serve.

2. **Slice Serve:** The slice serve involves hitting the ball with a side spin, causing the ball to curve to one side. This serve is useful for pulling opponents off the court and serving to the opponent's weaker side.

3. **Kick Serve:** The kick serve involves hitting the ball with topspin, causing the ball to bounce high and to the opposite side of the slice serve. This serve is particularly useful as a second serve due to its higher margin for error over the net.

Mastering the serve in tennis is essential for competitive play. The serve sets the tone for each point and can provide a significant advantage when executed correctly. Understanding the mechanics of the serve and the different serves can help players develop a reliable and effective serve.

Common Mistakes

Many players, especially those at the beginner and intermediate levels, often make certain mistakes that hinder their serving ability. Here are common mistakes made during tennis serving:

1. **Inconsistent Ball Toss**: An inconsistent ball toss is one of the most common mistakes in tennis serving. If the ball is tossed too low, it can lead to early contact and the ball hitting the net. On the other hand, if the ball is tossed too high, it can drop before contact is made, leading to a weak serve. A ball toss that varies in direction can disrupt the rhythm and timing of the serve.

2. **Incorrect Grip**: Using an incorrect grip while serving limits the serves a player can effectively execute. Many beginner players use a forehand or Eastern grip for serving, which limits their ability

to put a spin on the ball and can cause the serve to lack power and control. The Continental grip is generally recommended for serving because it allows a variety of serves, including flat, slice, and kick serves.

3. **Lack of Body Rotation and Leg Drive**: Another common mistake is not using the body and legs effectively during the serve. Some players rely too much on their arms to generate power, which not only leads to weak serves but also increases the risk of injuries. An effective serve should involve the whole body, with power generated from the ground up. It includes bending the knees to initiate the serve, rotating the torso during the swing, and driving up with the legs to transfer energy into the serve.

4. **Hitting the Ball Too Early or Too Late:** Hitting the ball too early or too late can result in a lack of power and control. The serve might lack power if the ball is hit too early before the racquet has completed its upward motion. If the ball is hit too late, after the racquet has started its downward motion, the serve might go long or lack control. The ideal point of contact is at the highest point of the ball toss, slightly in front of the body.

5. **Poor Follow-Through**: An incomplete or incorrect follow-through can affect the serve's accuracy, power, and spin. Ideally, the follow-through should involve the racquet continuing its motion down and across the body, finishing on the opposite side of the body. The server should also land inside the court, ready to respond to the return shot.

These common mistakes can significantly affect the effectiveness of a player's serve. Recognizing and addressing these mistakes, players significantly improve their serving ability and overall performance in tennis.

Practice Drills

Adeptness in tennis cannot be achieved without consistent and focused practice. Drills are excellent for honing skills, improving consistency, and increasing agility on the court. This section encompasses a number of drills to help players practice and refine their tennis fundamentals, whether practicing alone or with a partner.

1. **Cone Drill:** The cone drill is an excellent exercise for enhancing accuracy and control. Place a series of cones or markers on the other side of the net. The aim is to hit the cones with groundstrokes, alternating between forehand and backhand. This drill can be modified by varying the distance and placement of the cones.

2. **Wall Hitting Drill:** A wall-hitting drill can be performed solo, requiring only a wall and a ball. The player hits the ball against the wall, alternating between forehand and backhand shots. This drill is beneficial for improving stroke consistency and response time.

3. **Service Box Drill:** The service box drill is designed to improve serving accuracy. The player aims to serve the ball into the opposite service box, alternating between the deuce (right side) and ad (left side) court. The aim is to land as many serves as possible inside the service box.

4. **Cross-Court Drill:** The cross-court drill is performed with a partner. Players stand diagonally

across each other and exchange shots, aiming to keep the ball within the singles sideline and the service line. This drill develops control, consistency, and creating angles.

5. **Down-the-Line Drill**: Similar to the cross-court drill, the down-the-line drill is performed with a partner. However, players exchange shots down the line instead of cross-court in this drill. This drill helps improve precision and hitting straight shots.

6. **Approach-and-Volley Drill:** The approach-and-volley drill is perfect for practicing net play. One player feeds the ball, while the other player hits an approach shot and follows it to the net to volley the return. This drill improves transition to the net and volley skills.

7. **Baseline Rally Drill:** In the baseline rally drill, two players rally from the baseline, aiming to maintain the longest possible rally. This practice enhances consistency and endurance.

8. **Serve-and-Return Drill:** The serve-and-return drill is an excellent exercise for practicing the first few shots of a point. One player serves, the other player returns, and the server hits one more shot. This drill helps players work on their serve, return, and third shots.

These drills help players practice and refine the fundamental skills of tennis. Regular practice using these drills can significantly enhance a player's consistency, accuracy, control, and overall performance on the court.

Looking ahead, the next chapter builds upon these fundamentals, introducing players to more advanced techniques.

Chapter 4: Developing Your Technique

Improving your tennis technique is the cornerstone of becoming a more effective player. Your technique – how you hold your racket, move your feet, and swing to hit the ball – significantly influences your performance on the court. This chapter explains the importance of developing a sound tennis technique.

1. **Consistency**: When you have a strong technique, you can hit the ball more consistently. Accurately and dependably, returning the ball can often make the difference between winning and losing a match. Solid technique lets you control where and how the ball travels, making your shots more predictable and reliable.

2. **Power**: While strength and speed are key elements in generating power, your technique enables you to use these physical attributes fully. A well-executed swing can make the ball travel faster and further, allowing you to hit shots your opponent can't return.

3. **Precision:** Good technique allows you to hit the ball with precision. You will place the ball anywhere on the court, creating opportunities for strategic play, keeping your opponent guessing, and forcing them to move around, disrupting their rhythm and strategy.

4. **Injury Prevention**: Proper technique helps prevent injuries. Incorrect movements or posture can lead to strain and injury over time. For example, repeatedly serving with poor technique can lead to shoulder and elbow injuries. You can play safer and stay in the game longer with the proper technique.

5. **Stamina and Efficiency:** A sound technique is also energy efficient. Unnecessary movements or inefficient swings can drain your energy quickly, especially in long matches. A good technique enables you to use your energy more efficiently, conserving stamina for crucial moments in the match.

6. **Adaptability:** A solid technique provides a strong foundation for adapting to different situations in a game. Whether playing against a power-hitter or a tactician, on a slow clay court, or on a fast grass court, your technique helps you adjust your game accordingly.

Perfecting Your Groundstrokes

Groundstrokes in tennis are fundamental shots every player must master to compete effectively. They form the basis of the rally and are often the first line of offense and defense in a match. Groundstrokes are typically performed from the baseline, with the ball hit after it bounces once, using either a forehand or backhand stroke.

Consistently executing effective groundstrokes can grant a player significant control over rallies, allowing them to dictate the tempo and direction of the game. Well-executed groundstrokes can push opponents off-balance, opening up the court for attacking shots. Defensively, strong, deep groundstrokes can limit an opponent's offensive options, buying time to regain a balanced position on the court.

Moreover, groundstrokes are crucial to building physical stamina and enhancing coordination. The repetitive nature of these strokes helps improve muscle memory, promoting a fluid, efficient swing. The importance of groundstrokes in tennis is multifaceted, encompassing strategic, technical, and physical elements.

Basic Techniques for Forehand and Backhand Strokes

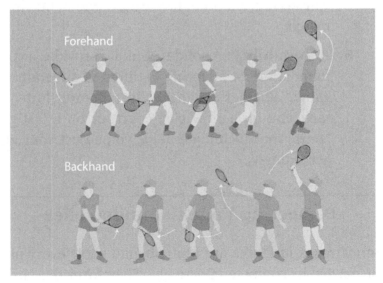

13. Forehand and backhand stroke techniques. Source:
https://cdn.britannica.com/21/62721-004-A2F958D2.gif

1. Forehand Stroke

The forehand is often the most powerful and frequently used groundstroke in tennis. Here are the basic elements to perfecting a forehand stroke:

- **Grip:** The most common grip for a forehand stroke is the Eastern or Semi-Western grip. These grips allow good balance of power and control.

- **Stance:** The player can use an open stance (facing the net), a semi-open stance, or a closed stance (sideways to the net). Each stance has advantages. Thee choice depends on the incoming ball and the desired shot.

- **Backswing:** The racket should move back in a smooth, circular motion. This coiling of the body stores energy released on the forward swing.

- **Contact:** Aim to hit the ball around waist height, slightly in front of the body. The racket face should be perpendicular to the court at the moment of contact.

- **Follow-through:** The follow-through should be a natural extension of the swing, with the racket ending high above the shoulder. It helps ensure good control and power.

2. Backhand Stroke

The backhand stroke can be hit with one or two hands on the racket. The two-handed backhand provides more power and control, while the one-handed backhand offers greater reach and variety. Here are the basics:

- **Grip:** For a two-handed backhand, the dominant hand (the hand at the bottom of the racket) uses an Eastern forehand grip, while the non-dominant hand uses an Eastern backhand grip. For a one-handed backhand, the Eastern backhand grip or Continental grip is commonly used.

- **Stance**: Similar to the forehand, the player can use an open, semi-open, or closed stance, depending on the situation.

- **Backswing:** For a two-handed backhand, the racket moves back with both hands on the handle, and the shoulders turn sideways. For a one-handed backhand, the backswing involves a shoulder turn, with the racket head rising above the level of the hand.

- **Contact**: The ball should be struck to the side of the body, with the racket face perpendicular to the net at the point of contact.

- **Follow-through**: A backhand's follow-through varies depending on whether it is one-handed or two-handed. For a two-handed backhand, both hands continue forward, with the racket finishing high. For a one-handed backhand, the follow-through typically has a high finish, with the racket pointing toward the target.

Perfecting your groundstrokes involves understanding and practicing these fundamental principles. With patience and practice, these techniques can become second nature, enabling you to control the game from the baseline and become a more formidable tennis player.

The Importance of Footwork and Body Positioning in Tennis

Footwork and body positioning are crucial components in tennis, complementing the technical aspects of stroke production. They are the bedrock upon which strong and effective groundstrokes are built. Therefore, their role in the sport cannot be understated.

Footwork is a player's steps and movements to reach the ball and deliver a stroke. The importance of footwork is linked to timing, balance, agility, and speed. Good footwork allows a player to be in the right place at the right time and hit the ball while maintaining balance. It also contributes to a player's ability to respond quickly and effectively to an opponent's shots.

Body positioning is the body's orientation relative to the ball at the point of contact. Proper body positioning ensures the player can optimally use their body's strength and leverage, delivering the stroke. It aids in maximizing power, control, and accuracy when hitting groundstrokes.

Drills for Improving Groundstrokes

Consistent practice through drills is key to perfecting groundstrokes. Here are some drills to help improve footwork, body positioning, and, consequently, the quality of groundstrokes.

1. **The Cone Drill:** This drill enhances speed, agility, and precision in footwork. Set up several cones in a straight line, each about two feet apart. The player must weave in and out of the cones as quickly as possible while controlling their movements. This drill can be combined with groundstroke practice by positioning a coach or a

ball machine to feed balls to the player after they complete the weaving pattern.

14. *The cone drill. Source: https://humankinetics.me/wp-content/uploads/2017/06/cone-slalom_brightcove-16x9_std.original.jpg*

2. **The Shadow Swing Drill:** This practice session improves body positioning and the fluidity of stroke mechanics. It involves the player performing shadow swings with their racket, focusing on maintaining the correct body position throughout the swing. This drill helps reinforce the proper technique without the distraction of an incoming ball.

3. **The Side-to-Side Drill**: This dynamic drill aims to improve court coverage and footwork. The player starts at the center of the baseline and runs to one side to hit a forehand, back to the center, and then to the other side to hit a backhand. This pattern is repeated for a set duration. This drill is effective for practicing groundstroke shots under movement and improving agility and endurance.

4. **The Depth Drill:** This drill is targeted at improving groundstroke depth and consistency. It involves hitting a series of forehands and backhands as deep into the opponent's court as possible. The player consistently aims to land the ball within a few feet of the baseline. This drill benefits players looking to improve their shot placement and control.

5. **The Wall Practice**: Wall practice is an excellent way to simultaneously work on groundstrokes, footwork, and body positioning. The player hits groundstrokes against a wall and focuses on moving their feet to position themselves correctly for each return. The speed of the rebound from the wall ensures the player gets a high-intensity workout and has to react quickly, like in a real match.

These drills can significantly improve a player's groundstrokes when practiced consistently. Improvement in tennis is often incremental and requires patience and persistence. With diligent practice, enhancing groundstrokes, footwork, and body positioning will invariably lead to better overall performance on the tennis court.

Enhancing Your Serve Technique

A potent serve is a powerful weapon in a tennis player's arsenal. It holds a unique position in tennis as the only shot where a player has complete control over how and when to play it. The importance of a strong and consistent serve cannot be overstated, as it sets the tone for each point and is significantly advantageous in a match.

A well-executed serve can seize the initiative right from the start of a rally, putting the opponent on the defensive or even winning points outright. It is a tool for dictating play, allowing the server to control the point strategically. A strong serve can alleviate pressure during crucial moments in a match, such as during tiebreaks or when facing break points.

Moreover, the serve's significance extends beyond its immediate impact on scoring points. A powerful and accurate serve can boost a player's confidence, disrupt the opponent's rhythm, and conserve energy by shortening points.

Basic Techniques for Serving

1. **Grip:** The grip is the foundation of a good serve. The most commonly used grip for serving is the Continental grip, sometimes called the "chopper" grip, because it resembles holding an axe. This grip allows a wide range of motion and generates spin. In this grip, the base knuckle of the index finger and the heel pad of the hand rest on the racquet handle's second bevel.

2. **Stance:** The stance is the position of the feet when preparing to serve. There are two primary stances: the platform stance and the pinpoint stance. In the platform stance, the feet are roughly shoulder-width apart throughout the serve. In the pinpoint stance, the back foot moves up to the front foot during the serve, "pinpointing" the feet together. Each stance has advantages, and the choice depends on what feels most comfortable and balanced for the player.

3. Motion

- **The Starting Position:** Hold the racquet with the chosen grip and stand in the preferred stance. The ball should be in the non-dominant hand, and the racquet in the dominant hand.

- **The Toss:** Toss the ball upward in front of your body. It should peak slightly to the right of the head (for right-handers) and slightly to the left for left-handers. The height of the toss should be just enough so the ball can be struck at full arm extension.

- **The Backswing:** As the ball is tossed, the racquet should be taken back in a motion often described as a "trophy pose." It requires bending the elbow and raising the racquet while the tossing arm extends upward.

- **The Strike:** As the ball descends from the toss, the player pushes up and forward with their legs and hips. The racquet swings up to meet the ball. Contact should be made with the ball at the highest possible point, with the arm fully extended.

- **The Follow-through:** After contact, the racquet should continue to move, following the direction of the serve. The body weight shifts forward into the court, with the player landing on their front foot.

Enhancing the serve technique involves meticulous attention to the grip, stance, and motion. With regular practice and focusing on the fundamentals, players can develop a strong, reliable serve, significantly elevating their overall performance in tennis.

Diversifying Your Serve

A variety of serves at your disposal can prove instrumental in disrupting an opponent's rhythm and gaining a strategic edge in a tennis match. The three primary serves are flat, slice, and kick, each with distinct characteristics and tactical implications.

1. **Flat Serve**: A flat serve is characterized by its speed and straight trajectory. The primary focus is on power, and the ball is hit with minimal spin, causing it to travel fast and straight. This serve can be advantageous when aiming for an ace or catching an opponent off guard. However, due to its lower margin for error, precision and control are crucial when executing a flat serve.

2. **Slice Serve**: A slice serve is identified by the sideways spin on the ball, causing it to curve to one side as it travels through the air. For right-handed players, a slice serve will curve to the left, while for left-handed players, it curves to the right. This serve can pull an opponent off the court, effectively opening up space for the following shot.

3. **Kick Serve:** A kick serve, known as a topspin serve, imparts significant topspin on the ball. The spin makes the ball bounce high and often to the opponent's opposite side - to the left for right-handers and to the right for left-handers. The kick serve is particularly useful as a second serve due to its high net clearance and deep bounce, which can keep the server in a safe, defensive position.

Drills for Improving Serve Technique

Numerous drills can be employed to improve and diversify the serve technique. Here are a few practical drills:

1. **Target Practice:** This drill places targets in different areas of the service box with the aim of hitting them. The targets can be moved around to practice different serves. For example, placing a target wide in the deuce court helps practice the slice serve for right-handers.

2. **Serve and Volley Drill**: This drill improves the serve and the transition to the net. The player serves and immediately moves forward to volley a return from a coach or partner. This drill helps improve the accuracy and placement of the serve and the footwork and timing for effective serve-and-volley play.

3. **Second Serve Drill:** Often a topspin or kick serve, this drill specifically improves the second serve. The player serves a series of second serves, focusing on imparting as much spin on the ball as possible. This practice helps increase the consistency and reliability of the second serve, reducing double faults.

4. **Serving Under Pressure**: This drill mimics the pressure of serving in a match situation. The player must serve a set number of successful serves in a row or achieve a certain number of serves in specific target areas. If the player fails, they start again from zero. This drill enhances mental toughness and serve reliability under pressure.

Players can significantly enhance their serve technique by understanding and practicing different serves and incorporating focused drills into training sessions. A diversified and reliable serve can be a formidable weapon on the tennis court, giving players the confidence and strategic flexibility to dictate play from the onset of a rally.

Mastering Net Play and Volleys

Net play is a fundamental tennis component that can transform a rally's dynamics. A proactive approach to net play often catches an opponent off guard, forcing them into a defensive position, and can be a game-changer in singles and doubles matches.

Mastering net play and volleys allows a player to reduce their opponent's reaction time, apply pressure, and control the pace and direction of the game. Furthermore, effective net play can open up opportunities for finishing points quickly, saving energy and reducing the duration of rallies.

A player adept at net play can diversify their game, making it difficult for opponents to anticipate their strategy. Net play is not solely about aggression; it's also a tactical tool adding versatility to a player's game.

Basic Techniques for Volleying and Approaching the Net

1. **Volleying:** Volleying involves hitting the ball before it bounces. Given the short reaction time, the emphasis is on quick reflexes and precise control rather than power. The two volley types are forehand and backhand, and the technique for both is a short, compact swing.

   For a forehand volley, the racquet should be held out front, slightly to the right for right-handed players and the left for left-handers. The racquet's face should be slightly open, and contact should be made in front

---

of the body. The backhand volley is similar, but the racquet is held slightly to the opposite side.

2. **Approaching the Net**: The approach to the net is often initiated by an approach shot, typically a deep, low shot aimed at the corners of the court. This shot forces the opponent to hit a defensive return, providing the server time to approach the net. As the player moves toward the net, it's crucial to maintain balance and be prepared to volley, either on the forehand or backhand side.

3. **Footwork and Positioning at the Net:** Footwork and positioning are critical aspects of effective net play. Split step, a small hop allowing a player to move quickly in any direction, is a vital footwork technique at the net. The split step should be timed so the player lands and is ready to move when the opponent strikes the ball.

Positioning at the net depends on various factors, including the opponent's position, the shot they're likely to hit, and the player's strengths and weaknesses. However, a general rule is to try and position yourself around the service line T, allowing coverage of the down-the-line and cross-court shots.

Drills for Improving Net Play and Volleys

1. **Mini Tennis Drill:** This drill involves playing points on a shortened court, typically between the service lines. It improves volley technique, reflexes, and touch and enhances control and timing.

2. **Volley to Volley Drill:** Two players stand at the net and continuously volley the ball to each other.

This drill improves reflexes, volley control, and consistency.

3. **Approach and Volley Drill:** A player hits an approach shot and then moves to the net to volley a return from a coach or partner. This drill enhances the transition from the baseline to the net, improves timing and footwork, and increases proficiency in executing volleys under pressure.

4. **Serve, Volley, and Put Away Drill:** The player serves, moves in for a volley, then tries to put away the next ball. This drill is excellent for players looking to incorporate serve-and-volley tactics into their game.

By understanding the importance of net play, mastering the basic techniques, and implementing focused drills, a player can significantly improve their performance at the net. Effective net play and volleys can add a new dimension to a player's game, offering a strategic advantage and making them a more versatile and formidable opponent on the tennis court.

The Importance of Specialty Shots in Tennis

Executing a variety of shots adds depth and versatility to a player's tennis game. Specialty shots like the slice, lob, and drop shots are strategic tools to disrupt the opponent's rhythm, create offensive opportunities, and provide defensive solutions. Players who skillfully employ these specialty shots can adjust their tactics according to the game situation and the opponent's playing style, enhancing their overall competitiveness on the court.

Basic Techniques

1. **Slice:** The slice shot is characterized by a backspin, causing the ball to move slower and bounce lower. The technique is a high-to-low swing path, with the racquet moving downward at the point of contact. The slicing action imparts a backspin on the ball, disrupting the pace of the rally and drawing the opponent out of their comfort zone.

2. **Lob:** The lob is a high, deep shot, often used as a defensive tool when a player is under pressure, particularly when the opponent is at the net. The racquet should make contact with the ball at a low-to-high angle, creating the necessary arc and spin. A well-executed lob can buy time to recover position or even win the point if it is out of the opponent's reach.

3. **Drop Shot:** The drop shot is a delicate, soft shot that barely clears the net and lands close to it on the opponent's side. The aim is to catch the opponent off guard and make them run forward, often leading to a winning point if executed well. The racquet should gently brush the ball in a high-to-low motion, producing a backspin and causing the ball to drop quickly after crossing the net.

When to Use Each Shot

The timing and decision to use each specialty shot are as crucial as the execution.

1. **Slice:** This shot is typically used to change the pace of the rally, forcing the opponent to generate their power. It is useful when returning a powerful

serve or shot, as the backspin can help control the pace and direction of the return.

2. **Lob:** The lob is most effective when the opponent is close to the net, like during a volley exchange or after an approach shot. It can also be a strategic choice when a player is out of position or under pressure.

3. **Drop Shot:** A drop shot can be a surprise tactic to exploit an opponent who tends to stay deep in the court. However, it requires precision and timing, as a poorly executed drop shot can present an easy opportunity for the opponent.

Drills for Mastering Specialty Shots

1. **Slice Practice:** Players can practice slice shots against a wall, focusing on creating a backspin and controlling the direction of the shot. Another drill involves a player feeding powerful shots and the other player returning them using only slice shots.

2. **Lob Over Obstacle**: Set up an obstacle near the net, like a tennis bag or cone. Players should aim to hit lobs over the obstacle and land them in the designated area. This drill will improve the trajectory and depth of the lob.

3. **Drop Shot Targets:** Place targets near the net in the service boxes. Players should aim to hit their drop shots onto these targets. This drill enhances the accuracy and feel required for effective drop shots.

Mastering specialty shots in tennis involves an understanding of their importance, learning the basic techniques, knowing when to use them, and regularly practicing in order to improve. Incorporating slice, lob, and drop shots into their repertoire, players add layers of complexity to their game, making them unpredictable and challenging opponents on the court.

Developing a Powerful and Accurate Return

The return of serve is a cornerstone of tennis strategy and is often considered the second most important shot after the serve. A strong and accurate return can neutralize an opponent's powerful serve, disrupt their rhythm, and immediately put them on the defensive. It can also set the tone for the rest of the rally, allowing the returner to seize control of the point early.

A well-executed return is a statement of intent, signaling the server that their serve can be challenged and every point will be fiercely contested. Therefore, developing a powerful and accurate return is critical for a player wishing to elevate their game and become a formidable competitor.

Basic Techniques for Returning a Serve

The returning serve effectively demands a blend of technical skills, including rapid reaction, precise timing, and correct body positioning.

1. **Reaction and Timing:** Reacting quickly to the serve and timing the return accurately are both essential to return the serve successfully. The returner must read the server's body language, racket movement, and ball toss to anticipate the type and direction of the serve. This anticipation, with quick reflexes, can help the returner position themselves and time their return effectively.

2. **Body Positioning:** The returner should maintain a balanced and slightly crouched stance for

forehand and backhand returns, ready to move in any direction. Given the limited reaction time, the racket must be taken back early with a compact swing. The strike should be clean, with the returner focusing on using the server's pace to their advantage rather than trying to generate excessive power.

Footwork and Positioning When Returning Serve

Footwork and positioning play integral roles in developing a powerful and accurate return.

1. **Footwork:** Good footwork can enhance the returner's ability to react quickly to the serve. The split step, a small hop that allows a player to move quickly in any direction, is vital when returning serve. It should be timed so the player lands and is ready to move when the opponent strikes the ball.

2. **Positioning**: The returner's position depends largely on the server's style and the serve type anticipated. However, a general rule is standing wider from the center mark for a first serve, allowing a better chance to return powerful, wide serves. For second serves, the returner may stand closer to the center mark to apply pressure on the server by showing intent to attack a weaker serve.

Drills for Improving Return Technique

1. **Rapid Fire Return Drill**: A coach or hitting partner serves continuously to the returner, alternating between the forehand and backhand sides in this drill. The returner focuses on reacting quickly, maintaining proper form, and placing the return accurately. This drill enhances reaction speed, timing, and accuracy.

2. **Serve Return with Target Areas**: Place target areas in the service box where the returner aims to direct their return. This drill improves precision in return placement and develops control over the return direction.

3. **Serve and Rally Drill**: A player serves, and the returner attempts to initiate a rally with their return. The aim is to return the serve to facilitate a neutral or advantageous rally situation for the returner.

The return of serve is a critical aspect of tennis that can significantly influence the outcome of a match. It requires fast reflexes, precise timing, effective footwork, and accurate shot placement. Understanding the importance of a strong return, mastering the basic techniques, and employing focused drills, a player develops a powerful and accurate return, adding a potent weapon to their tennis arsenal.

Mental Aspects of Technique Development

In the thrilling sport of tennis, mental focus is as critical as physical prowess, particularly in technique development. Mental focus enables a player to concentrate on the intricacies of a particular tennis stroke, perceive subtleties, and make necessary adjustments.

The mental aspect helps grasp complex movements, breaking them down into achievable segments and seamlessly integrating them into a coordinated overall motion. A heightened mental focus is essential for receptivity to feedback. Feedback, internal (like the feel of the racket in the hand or the body's movement) and external (a coach's insight or video analysis), is crucial for refining and perfecting tennis techniques.

Visualization and Mental Imagery Techniques in Tennis

Visualization and mental imagery are potent tools in a tennis player's arsenal. These cognitive strategies involve mentally rehearsing a tennis stroke or movement without physically performing it. This mental practice can reinforce neural pathways related to the execution of that particular stroke, complementing physical practice.

The imagination should be thorough, incorporating as many senses as possible. A player could visualize the racket's grip, the sound of the ball hitting the racket, their precise movements, their footwork, and the ball's trajectory. Regular mental imagery practice enhances understanding of the technique, bolsters confidence, and improves the execution of strokes on the court.

Dealing with Mistakes and Setbacks in Tennis

Mistakes and setbacks are inherent parts of the journey toward mastery in tennis. How a player mentally handles these can significantly influence their progress in technique development.

A constructive approach is to view mistakes as learning opportunities rather than failures. This shift in perception promotes a growth mindset, fostering resilience and encouraging continued effort toward improvement. Instead of becoming disheartened by a missed shot, players should analyze what led to the mistake, identify areas for improvement, and devise a strategy to rectify it.

Setbacks, like plateaus in progress or temporary performance declines, require patience and perseverance.

Rather than inducing stress, these periods should be opportunities to consolidate skills, address weaknesses, and build mental fortitude.

Tips for Staying Motivated during Tennis Practice

Preserving motivation is vital for continuous engagement and long-term progress in technique development in tennis. Here are several strategies:

1. **Set Clear Goals:** Establishing specific, measurable, achievable, relevant, and time-bound (SMART) goals can provide direction, enhance motivation, and create accomplishment.

2. **Celebrate Small Wins**: Acknowledging and celebrating progress, even minor improvements, can boost motivation and enjoyment in learning.

3. **Maintain a Positive Attitude:** A positive mindset can fuel motivation, increase enjoyment of the sport, and improve resilience in challenges.

4. **Vary Practice Routines:** Mixing up practice routines or changing practice environments can keep the process interesting, stimulating, and enjoyable, enhancing motivation.

The mental aspects of technique development in tennis are integral facets of the game, significantly influencing a player's performance. Understanding the importance of mental focus, implementing visualization techniques, adopting a constructive approach to mistakes, and employing strategies to maintain motivation, tennis players boost their technique development journey, leading to greater proficiency, enjoyment, and success on the court.

Chapter 5: Strategy and Tactics

The significance of strategy and tactics extends far beyond mere proficiency with racket and ball in tennis. In essence, they form the intellectual backbone of the sport, dictating the course of matches and the trajectory of careers. Without a deep understanding and application of strategies and tactics, even players with the strongest serves or the most powerful forehands could find themselves consistently outmaneuvered by more strategic opponents.

The Interplay between Strategy and Tactics

Strategy and tactics in tennis are two sides of the same coin, intertwined yet distinct. Strategy refers to a player's overarching game plan, considering their strengths and weaknesses and the opponent's. It is a long-term perspective, a vision of how the match ought to unfold.

On the other hand, tactics are the specific, immediate actions taken on the court to implement the strategy. They are the individual decisions made in the heat of the moment, the split-second adjustments that could tip the balance of a point, a game, or even a set.

Importance of Strategy

Strategy in tennis is the roadmap guiding a player's actions throughout a match. It considers the player's skillset, the opponent's playing style, and the conditions of the game.

A sound strategy allows players to maximize their strengths and exploit their opponent's weaknesses. It can guide a player toward choosing the right shots at the right time, managing energy levels, and controlling the tempo and rhythm of the match. Without a solid strategy, a player might falter, reacting instead of acting and allowing the opponent to dictate the game's pace.

Importance of Tactics

On the other hand, tactics are the tools that bring a strategy to life. They are a player's specific actions and decisions in real-time to gain an advantage. These include when to rush the net, play a drop shot, or aim for the lines.

Effective tactics require physical skill and a high degree of mental agility. Players must quickly assess the situation, decide, and adjust their play accordingly. This ability to think on your feet and adapt tactics responding to the unfolding game is a hallmark of the best players in tennis.

Understanding Court Positioning

The tennis court is a battlefield, each section bearing strategic significance. Mastery of court positioning relies on a deep understanding of these areas and their potential advantages.

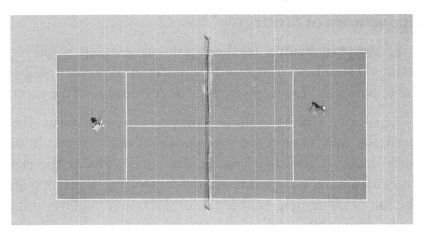

15. Each section of a tennis court has strategic significance. Source: https://unsplash.com/photos/aG6ByqGXiXg?utm_source=unsplash&utm_medium=referral&utm_content=creditShareLink

1. **Baseline:** At the furthest ends of the court, the baseline is a sanctuary for defensive players and power hitters. Here, players benefit from increased reaction time, offering opportunities to return powerful serves and groundstrokes. Yet, it is also a platform for aggressive play, allowing powerful shots to dominate rallies.

2. **Net:** In stark contrast to the baseline, the net area is the zone for aggressive, offensive play. Players can execute quick volleys, sharp-angled shots, and decisive put-aways here. However, the proximity to the net requires swift reflexes and accurate timing.

3. **Service Boxes**: The four service boxes between the net and the baseline are the starting points for each point in a game. These areas are also the target for strategic plays like drop shots and slices that aim to draw opponents forward, disrupting their positioning.

4. **Alleys:** The alleys, known as the tramlines, are the outermost sections of the court. While typically out-of-bounds in singles play, these areas become vital zones of strategic play in doubles matches. Skillful exploitation of the alleys can stretch the opposing team, creating openings in their defense.

The Importance of Maintaining Proper Positioning

Maintaining proper positioning on the court is pivotal to a player's success. It is a balancing act, navigating between attack and defense, exertion and conservation, and aggression and restraint.

Proper positioning confers several advantages:

1. **Anticipation:** Adequate positioning enables players to predict and react more efficiently to opponents' shots.

2. **Control:** It facilitates greater control over the rally, allowing players to execute a wider range of shots and manipulate the opponent's movements.

3. **Energy Conservation:** Efficient positioning minimizes unnecessary movements, conserving energy for critical points in the match.

Tips for Moving Efficiently on Court

Effective court coverage is a blend of anticipation, speed, and efficient footwork. Here are some tips:

1. **Split Step**: A small hop a player performs as their opponent hits the ball, preparing for immediate movement in any direction.

2. **Cross-Over Steps:** For covering longer distances, cross-over steps (one foot crossing over

the other) can be quicker and more efficient than side-stepping or running.

3. **Recovery Steps:** Post hitting a shot, players should use recovery steps to swiftly return to an optimal, balanced position.

4. **Anticipation:** Anticipating the opponent's shots and starting movement before the shot is made gives a significant advantage.

5. **Physical Conditioning**: Proper court coverage demands speed, endurance, and agility. Regular fitness training should be integral to a player's routine to enhance these attributes.

Court positioning is a strategic fulcrum of tennis. It demands physical prowess and a keen understanding of the game dynamics, the opponent's tendencies, and the player's capabilities. Mastering this element can significantly elevate the player's game, giving them a substantial edge in competitive play.

Developing a Tennis Game Plan

Stepping onto the tennis court without a game plan is akin to embarking on a journey without a map. A well-thought-out strategy gives direction and focus, guiding a player's decision-making throughout the match. It enables them to play proactively rather than reactively, dictating the game's flow rather than at the mercy of the opponent's actions.

A game plan is not merely about winning. It is a tool for personal improvement, helping players identify and leverage their strengths while working on their weaknesses. In short, a game plan is a rudder that steers the ship, providing structure, purpose, and a path to victory.

Developing a Game Plan Based on Personal Strengths and Weaknesses

Creating an effective game plan is a process of self-awareness and tactical consideration. It begins with a candid assessment of your abilities and limitations.

1. **Assessing Strengths and Weaknesses**: Every player possesses unique skills and limitations. Some have a powerful serve or a deadly forehand, while others excel in endurance or court coverage. Identifying these strengths and weaknesses is the first step in developing a game plan.

2. **Analyzing the Opponent:** In addition to understanding your game, it is equally important to study the opponent. Observing their playing style, identifying their strengths and weaknesses, and remembering past encounters provide valuable insight that shapes the game plan.

3. **Formulating the Plan:** Once the player's strengths and weaknesses and those of the opponent are clear, the next step is to formulate a strategy, maximizing the player's advantages and exploiting the opponent's vulnerabilities. It could be focusing on baseline rallies if endurance is a strength or frequently serving wide to exploit a weak backhand return from the opponent.

Tips for Adjusting a Game Plan During a Match

Despite the best-laid plans, the unpredictable nature of tennis often necessitates adjustments mid-match. Here are some tips for adapting a game plan on the fly:

1. **Observe and Adapt**: Continuously observe the opponent's strategies and tendencies. Be ready to

adjust the game plan if the opponent counters effectively or changes their strategy.

2. **Stay Flexible**: Flexibility is key. If a strategy isn't working, don't hesitate to revise it. Remember, stubbornly sticking to a failing plan usually leads to defeat.

3. **Use Time Wisely**: Use changeovers and breaks to assess the match's progress, identify what's working and what's not, and tweak the game plan accordingly.

4. **Consult a Coach:** If available, consult with a coach during breaks. They can provide an external perspective and valuable advice on adjusting the game plan.

5. **Trust Instincts:** Sometimes, instincts provide the best guidance. If something feels right, it may be worth incorporating into the game plan, even if it wasn't part of the original strategy.

Analyzing Opponents and Exploiting Weaknesses

In the game of tennis, knowledge is power. Understanding an opponent's strengths, weaknesses, and tendencies is crucial to formulating an effective strategy. By studying opponents, players can anticipate their moves, exploit their weaknesses, and disrupt their game plan.

Studying opponents begins long before stepping onto the court. It encompasses reviewing past match footage, researching their performance statistics, and observing their pre-match routines and demeanor. This comprehensive approach provides a wealth of information that can be harnessed to gain a strategic edge.

How to Analyze an Opponent's Playing Style and Tendencies

Analyzing an opponent's playing style and tendencies involves a systematic approach. Here are some key aspects to consider:

1. **Technical Proficiency:** Examine the opponent's technical skills. How strong are their serves, forehands, and backhands? Do they prefer groundstrokes, or are they more comfortable at the net? Understanding these aspects can reveal potential weaknesses to exploit.

2. **Tactical Preferences:** Observe the opponent's tactical preferences. Do they favor baseline rallies or aggressive net play? Are they more defensive or offensive? Identifying these patterns can help anticipate their moves during the match.

3. **Physical and Mental Fortitude:** Assess the opponent's physical and mental stamina. Are they quick and agile, or do they tire easily? How do they respond to pressure situations? These insights guide the strategy for long rallies and critical points.

4. **Patterns of Play:** Look for patterns in the opponent's play, like favored serve placements or repetitive shot sequences. Once recognized, these tendencies can be anticipated and countered effectively.

Tips for Exploiting an Opponent's Weaknesses During a Match

Once an opponent's weaknesses have been identified, the next challenge is to exploit them effectively during the match. Here are some tips:

1. **Play to the Weaknesses:** Regularly hit shots to the opponent's weaker side. For example, if the opponent has a weaker backhand, keep directing the ball to that side to exert pressure.

2. **Disrupt Rhythms:** If the opponent prefers a certain pace or rhythm, try to disrupt it. For example, a mix of fast and slow or high and low balls to keep them guessing.

3. **Test Endurance**: If endurance is a weakness for the opponent, aim for long rallies to wear them down.

4. **Apply Pressure:** If the opponent cracks under pressure, create high-pressure situations. For instance, play aggressively at crucial points or show no signs of fatigue or frustration.

5. **Adapt and Adjust:** Always be ready to adjust tactics based on the opponent's responses. If they counter a strategy effectively, quickly switch to another tactic.

Singles Strategies for Winning Matches

In singles tennis, your abilities and tactics are the sole determinants of success. Therefore, playing to personal strengths becomes paramount. By focusing on areas of proficiency, players can dictate the flow of the match, keeping the opponent on the defensive and controlling the game's tempo. Whether a powerful serve, a precise volley, or unyielding stamina, leveraging these strengths forms the cornerstone of a successful singles strategy.

Tips for Serving Effectively

The serve is the only shot in tennis where a player has complete control, making it a critical weapon in singles play. Here are some tips for serving effectively:

1. **Mix-Up Serves**: Vary the speed, spin, and direction of serves to keep the opponent guessing. Mixing up serves not only keeps the opponent off balance but also prevents them from getting comfortable with a particular return.

2. **Aim for High First Serve Percentage**: A high first serve percentage puts immediate pressure on the opponent and minimizes exposure to the vulnerabilities of a second serve. Accuracy and consistency should be emphasized over power in most situations.

3. **Practice Placement Over Power:** While a powerful serve can be an asset, accurate placement often yields higher dividends. A well-placed serve can pull the opponent out of position, opening the court for the next shot.

Strategies for Returning Serves

Returning serves effectively is just as important as serving well. Here are some strategies for handling an opponent's serves:

1. **Anticipate the Serve:** Look for cues in the server's body language or serving patterns to anticipate the direction and serve type. Getting a jump on the serve can turn defense into offense.

2. **Attack the Second Serve:** Second serves are typically slower and less precise, providing an opportunity to seize the offensive. Use aggressive returns to put the server on the back foot from the outset.

3. **Aim for Deep Returns:** Returning the serve deep in the court limits the server's options for the next shot, neutralizing their advantage and buying time to get into an optimal position for the next shot.

Tips for Playing Aggressively and Defensively

Balancing aggressive and defensive play is a key aspect of singles strategy. Here are some tips:

1. **Aggressive Play**

   - **Seize the Offensive:** Take control of the point early by attacking vulnerable returns and capitalizing on short balls.

   - **Approach the Net**: Following strong groundstrokes, quickly approach the net to finish points with volleys or overheads.

   - **Target the Lines:** Hitting close to the lines can stretch the opponent and open up the court for subsequent shots.

2. **Defensive Play**

   - **Use the Lob:** A well-executed lob can neutralize net approaches, buying time to regain a balanced position.

   - **Hit Deep Groundstrokes:** Deep groundstrokes can push the opponent back, preventing them from attacking.

- **Maintain Patience:** In defensive scenarios, patience is crucial. Rather than attempting risky shots, focus on returning the ball consistently and wait for an opportunity to switch back to the offense.

Doubles Strategies: Effective Communication and Teamwork

Unlike singles tennis, "doubles" is played as a partnership. Effective communication and seamless teamwork are the lifeblood of a successful doubles team. From coordinating serve-and-volley tactics to determining who takes the shot in the middle of the court, every move is a complex dance requiring clear communication and mutual understanding. A well-coordinated team can often outplay opponents with superior individual skills, underscoring the importance of teamwork in doubles tennis.

Strategies for Serving and Returning Serves in Doubles

Serving and returning serves in doubles involves unique strategies leveraging the presence of a partner. Here are some tips:

1. **Serving**

   - **Coordinate with Partner**: Before serving, discuss strategies with your partner. For instance, one player could decide to serve wide, and the partner covers the down-the-line return.

   - **Serve to Weaknesses:** Unlike singles, serving in doubles often targets an opponent's weaker player or the weaker return side, exploiting vulnerabilities to gain an immediate advantage.

- **Maintain Consistency**: Double faults are especially costly, as they give away points without the opponents having to play. Consistency in serving is crucial.

2. **Returning Serves**

- **Communicate:** Before the point, the receiving team should communicate their intentions. If the receiver plans to return down the line, the partner should be ready to cover the net.

- **Attack the Server's Partner**: Returns targeting the server's partner can put immediate pressure on the opponents, disrupting their game plan.

- **Aim for Low Returns:** Low returns can force the server's partner to hit up, offering the receiving team an opportunity to attack.

Tips for Effective Movement and Positioning in Doubles

Positioning and movement in doubles are radically different from singles because four players are on the court. Here are some tips:

1. **Move as a Unit**: Teammates should move in sync, like two sides of a rectangle moving together. If one player moves to the net, the other should follow, and vice versa.

2. **Cover the Middle**: The area down the middle is a common target in doubles. Players should position themselves to cover this area effectively.

3. **Balance Aggression and Caution at the Net:** Playing at the net can be advantageous, allowing for aggressive volleys. However, it also exposes the team to passing shots and lobs. Balance is key.

How to Develop Synergy with a Doubles Partner

Developing synergy with a doubles partner requires time, practice, and understanding. Here are some strategies:

1. **Communicate Effectively**: Clear, constant communication is crucial. Discuss strategies openly, and always signal before serving.

2. **Understand Each Other's Games**: Know each other's strengths, weaknesses, and tendencies. This understanding helps strategize and anticipate each other's moves.

3. **Practice Together:** Spend time practicing as a team to build understanding and coordination. Execute drills focusing on doubles skills like poaching, alley shots, and coordinated net play.

Chapter 6: Fitness and Conditioning for Tennis

This chapter explores the essential aspect of tennis that often goes unnoticed by the casual spectator yet is integral to every facet of the game: fitness and conditioning. The importance of physical fitness in tennis cannot be overstated. It is the bedrock upon which the skills and strategies of the sport rest.

Tennis is a physically demanding sport requiring a unique combination of aerobic stamina, anaerobic fitness, power, agility, speed, and flexibility. It requires players to maintain high intensity over an extended period, often several hours. It involves short bursts of sprinting, frequent direction changes, and a continuous cycle of loading and unloading the muscles during shots.

Furthermore, the physical demands of tennis vary greatly due to playing style, match duration, surface type, and environmental conditions. Hence, tennis players require a comprehensive, well-rounded fitness regime, preparing them for all possible scenarios.

Importance of Physical Fitness for Tennis

16. Maintaining physical fitness will help you play better. Source: https://unsplash.com/photos/oGv9xIl7DkY?utm_source=unsplash &utm_medium=referral&utm_content=creditShareLink

Physical fitness in tennis implies a multifaceted spectrum of physical capabilities enabling a player to perform optimally. It includes endurance, strength, speed, agility, flexibility, and power, contributing to a player's overall performance on the court.

1. **Endurance:** Endurance in tennis refers to aerobic and anaerobic fitness. Aerobic fitness allows players to maintain steady performance over extended periods, which is crucial in long matches. Anaerobic fitness is needed for the short, intense bursts of activity characterizing many tennis points, like sprinting to reach a drop shot or leaping for an overhead smash.

2. **Strength:** Strength in tennis is not about muscle bulk but rather functional strength; the strength that helps players hit powerful shots, maintain stability during quick movements, and endure the demands of a tough match. Core strength is particularly important, as a strong core helps improve balance, provides stability, and aids efficient energy transfer from the lower to the upper body during strokes.

3. **Speed and Agility:** Speed is a critical attribute for reaching the ball in time, while agility allows players to change direction quickly and efficiently. Together, these qualities enable players to respond to opponents' shots effectively, no matter how fast or unpredictable.

4. **Flexibility:** Flexibility aids in a wide range of motion, which is essential for executing various tennis strokes. It also helps prevent injuries by reducing the strain on muscles and joints.

5. **Power:** Power is exerting maximum force in short intervals. In tennis, this translates to hitting strong serves and groundstrokes and often stems from combined strength and speed.

Benefits of Physical Fitness for Tennis Players

Physical fitness offers a plethora of benefits for tennis players. These include:

1. **Enhanced Performance**: A fit player can reach the ball faster, hit harder, last longer, and recover quicker than an unfit opponent. It can distinguish between winning and losing, especially in close matches.

2. **Injury Prevention:** A well-conditioned body is less likely to get injured. Strength training can fortify muscles and tendons, flexibility exercises improve joint mobility and muscle elasticity, and endurance training enhances overall resilience.

3. **Improved Recovery**: Fit players recover more quickly between points, games, and matches, allowing them to maintain high performance throughout a match and bounce back more quickly after strenuous contests.

4. **Mental Toughness:** Physical fitness contributes to mental toughness. The confidence that comes from knowing your body can endure the demands of the game can give players an important psychological edge, helping them stay focused and resilient under pressure.

Warm-Up and Cool-Down Exercises

Warm-up exercises are indispensable in preparing the body for the physical demands of tennis. They gradually increase the heart rate, boost blood flow to the muscles, loosen joints, and enhance coordination. They help prevent injuries and improve performance.

Warm-Up Exercises for Tennis Players

A comprehensive warm-up for tennis is a mix of cardiovascular exercises, dynamic stretches, and sport-specific drills. Here are some examples:

1. **Cardiovascular Exercises:** A light jog or cycling helps increase the heart rate and warms the muscles. This exercise should ideally last for about 5 to 10 minutes.

2. **Dynamic Stretches:** Dynamic stretches involve moving parts of the body to increase reach and speed of movement gradually. They include leg swings, arm circles, and torso twists.

DYNAMIC STRETCHES

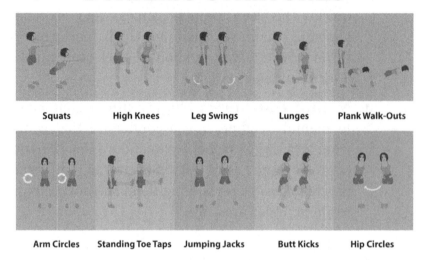

17. *Dynamic stretches involve moving parts of the body to increase speed and reach. Source:*
https://www.atipt.com/sites/default/files/201229_Blog_JanSupportingBlogPostInfographics_Dynamic.jpg

3. **Sport-Specific Drills:** These exercises mimic the movements in tennis, helping players prepare for the match. They include shadow swings, mini tennis, and agility ladder drills.

The Importance of Cool-Down Exercises

Like a proper warm-up helps prepare the body for a match, a good cool-down helps the body recover after one. It allows the heart rate and blood pressure to return to normal gradually, removes lactic acid buildup, and reduces post-exercise muscle soreness. Furthermore, a cool-down improves flexibility and speeds up recovery.

Cool-Down Exercises for Tennis Players

A good cool-down routine for tennis players should involve light cardiovascular exercise and static stretching:

1. **Light Cardiovascular Exercise:** A slow jog or walk for about 5 to 10 minutes lowers the heart rate gradually.

2. **Static Stretching:** Static stretching involves holding a stretch for 20-30 seconds. It improves flexibility, relaxes the muscles, and speeds up recovery. These stretches should target all major muscle groups used in tennis, such as the calves, hamstrings, quads, glutes, core, shoulders, and forearms.

Strength and Conditioning Training

Strength and conditioning training for tennis players refers to a structured and targeted exercise regimen to build functional strength and improve overall physical conditioning. This training focuses on enhancing the specific attributes required for tennis, such as power, agility, speed, endurance, and flexibility.

Strength training usually involves resistance exercises targeting the major muscle groups in tennis strokes, such as the legs, core, and upper body. The aim is not to build bulky muscles but to enhance functional strength and power, contributing to faster, more explosive movements and harder shots on the court.

Conditioning training focuses on improving the cardiovascular and metabolic systems to enhance endurance and recovery. It often combines aerobic exercises (like long-distance running) for long-term stamina and anaerobic exercises (like sprinting or high-intensity interval training) for short-term, high-intensity efforts.

Benefits of Strength and Conditioning Training for Tennis Players

Strength and conditioning training offer several benefits for tennis players:

1. **Improved Performance:** Improved strength leads to more powerful serves and groundstrokes, while better conditioning enhances speed, agility, and endurance on the court.

2. **Injury Prevention**: Stronger muscles, tendons, and ligaments are more resilient and less prone to injuries. Conditioning exercises, especially those improving flexibility and balance, help prevent injuries by enhancing body control and reducing falls and awkward movements.

3. **Faster Recovery:** Better conditioning allows quicker recovery during (between points and games) and after a match. It is significantly advantageous in long matches or tournaments with limited recovery time between matches.

4. **Enhanced Longevity in the Sport**: Regular strength and conditioning training helps players maintain high physical fitness and continue playing tennis competitively for longer periods.

Strength and Conditioning Exercises

1. Strength Exercises

Strength exercises for tennis players often involve resistance training. Some effective exercises include:

- **Lunges and Squats:** These exercises strengthen the lower body and core, which is crucial for powerful groundstrokes and serve.

18. Squats strengthen the lower body. Source: https://unsplash.com/photos/wy_L8WozcpI?utm_source=unsplash&utm_medium=referral&utm_content=creditShareLink

- **Planks and Russian Twists**: These exercises target the core, enhancing stroke stability and rotational strength.

- **Push-Ups and Pull-Ups:** These exercises strengthen the upper body, which is essential for serves, volleys, and overhead smashes.

19. Push-ups can strengthen the upper body. Source: https://unsplash.com/photos/wy_L8WozcpI?utm_source=unsplas h&utm_medium=referral&utm_content=creditShareLink

2. Conditioning Exercises

Conditioning exercises for tennis players should include aerobic and anaerobic workouts. Some examples are:

- **Long-Distance Running or Cycling**: These are effective aerobic exercises that improve overall stamina.

- **Sprint Intervals:** These anaerobic exercises enhance speed and quick, explosive movements.

- **Agility Drills**: Exercises like ladder drills or zig-zag sprints improve agility, which is crucial for changing directions quickly during a match.

Agility and Speed Training

Agility and speed training for tennis players aims to enhance their ability to move quickly and change directions efficiently on the court. Tennis is a sport requiring not only linear but also lateral and diagonal movements, often at high speed under challenging conditions.

Speed training typically focuses on improving a player's ability to move quickly in a straight line. It is particularly beneficial when chasing down a ball or reaching the net in as little time as possible.

Agility training focuses on enhancing a player's ability to change direction rapidly without losing balance or speed. This skill is crucial when players have to adjust their movements to respond to their opponent's shots.

Benefits of Agility and Speed Training for Tennis Players

Agility and speed training offers several benefits for tennis players:

1. **Enhanced Court Coverage:** Improved speed helps players reach more balls during a match. Enhanced agility enables them to change direction quickly, allowing them to respond effectively to a wider range of shots.

2. **Improved Offensive and Defensive Skills:** Faster and more agile players get to the ball earlier, giving them more time to prepare for their shot and more offensive and defensive options.

3. **The Advantage in Long Matches**: Agility and speed offer significant advantages in long matches,

where slower, less agile players struggle to maintain their performance.

4. **Reduced Injury Risk:** Agility training contributes to injury prevention by improving balance and body control, reducing the risk of falls and awkward movements.

Agility and Speed Training Exercises

1. Speed Exercises

Speed exercises for tennis players often involve sprinting workouts, such as:

- **Straight-Line Sprints:** Sprinting in a straight line for a short distance, followed by a short recovery period.

- **Suicide Drills:** Sprinting to various points on the court and back in quick succession.

2. Agility Exercises

Agility exercises for tennis players typically involve drills mimicking the movements required in a match. Some examples include:

- **Ladder Drills:** Running through agility ladders in various patterns enhances foot speed and agility.

- **Cone Drills:** Weaving around a series of cones improves the ability to change direction quickly.

- **Shadow Drills:** Mimicking the movement patterns of different strokes without hitting a ball enhances agility and muscle memory.

Common Injuries in Tennis

Like all sports, tennis carries the risk of injuries due to its physical demands. Some of the most common injuries among tennis players include:

1. **Tennis Elbow**: Tennis elbow, or lateral epicondylitis, is a painful condition when the tendons in the elbow are overloaded, usually by repetitive motions of the wrist and arm. The pain mainly occurs when the forearm muscles' tendons attach to the bony bump on the outside of the elbow.

2. **Shoulder Injuries**: The repetitive and high-speed shoulder movements during tennis, especially when serving and hitting overheads, can lead to numerous shoulder injuries. These include rotator cuff injuries, impingement syndrome, and shoulder instability.

3. **Ankle Sprains:** Quick, side-to-side movements and rapid changes in direction lead to ankle sprains. This injury occurs when the ankle rolls inward or outward unnaturally, stretching or tearing the ligaments.

4. **Stress Fractures:** Stress fractures are small cracks in a bone occurring over time due to repetitive force, often from overuse like repeatedly jumping up and down or running long distances.

Tips for Injury Prevention

While injuries in tennis are common, players can employ several strategies to minimize their risk:

1. **Physical Conditioning**: Regular strength and conditioning training enhances muscle strength

and flexibility, reducing the risk of injuries. It's important to focus on all the major muscle groups involved in tennis, not only the most common ones.

2. **Proper Technique**: Using the correct technique for all tennis strokes prevents overuse and strain injuries. Taking lessons from a certified coach who can guide proper technique is often beneficial.

3. **Adequate Warm-Up and Cool-Down:** As discussed earlier, a proper warm-up and cool-down routine prepares the muscles for activity and aids in recovery, reducing the risk of injuries.

4. **Regular Rest**: Rest is crucial for recovery and injury prevention. Overtraining can lead to fatigue and increase the risk of injuries.

Techniques for Injury Recovery

In the event of an injury, the following recovery techniques aid in healing and returning to the sport:

1. **Rest, Ice, Compression, and Elevation (RICE):** The RICE method is a simple self-care technique that helps reduce swelling, ease pain, and speed up healing.

2. **Physical Therapy:** Physical therapy can restore function to injured areas and strengthen muscles to prevent future injuries.

3. **Surgery**: In severe cases, surgery is necessary to repair damaged areas. It is usually followed by a period of physical therapy.

4. **Gradual Return to Play**: Once recovered from an injury, returning to play gradually is important,

starting with light drills before moving on to more intense practice and match play.

Injuries are common in tennis, but they can often be prevented with proper physical conditioning, technique, warm-up and cool-down routines, and rest. If an injury occurs, techniques such as the RICE method, physical therapy, and surgery will aid recovery. Returning to play gradually to prevent re-injury is crucial.

Chapter 7: Tennis Etiquette and Sportsmanship

Beyond being a game of skill, agility, and strategy, tennis is also a game of respect. The etiquette and sportsmanship customs that have evolved with the sport are as important as the game's rules.

Tennis etiquette and sportsmanship encompass a wide range of behaviors, on and off the court, contributing to creating a fair, enjoyable, and respectful environment for all participants. It includes the players, officials, and spectators. Tennis etiquette and sportsmanship principles uphold the sport's integrity, promote fair competition, and foster camaraderie and mutual respect among players.

Adherence to these principles reflects not only on a player's character but also their understanding of the game. Ignoring or violating these principles can disrupt the game flow, create a hostile environment, and result in penalties or disqualification.

This chapter explains the importance of tennis etiquette and sportsmanship, exploring their various aspects and how they contribute to the game's overall experience.

Tennis etiquette is unwritten rules or conventions governing behavior on the tennis court. These guidelines, which extend beyond the formal rules of the game, dictate how players should conduct themselves to maintain a respectful and sportsmanlike atmosphere. They encompass a broad range of actions and behaviors, from how players interact with their opponent, umpire, and spectators to how they handle victory or defeat.

The History of Tennis Etiquette

With its origins dating back to the 12th century, tennis has a long and illustrious history. It started as a game for European royalty and was affectionately known as the "sport of kings." Due to its royal roots, tennis naturally adopted a code of conduct befitting the noble courts, which eventually transformed into today's tennis etiquette.

In the early days, tennis was as much a social event as a sporting competition. As a result, players were expected to behave in a manner reflecting well on themselves and their noble status. It involved showing respect for their opponents, refraining from unsportsmanlike behavior, and maintaining a dignified demeanor, irrespective of the match's outcome.

Over the centuries, as the sport evolved and became more accessible to the masses, so did its code of conduct. Nevertheless, the emphasis on sportsmanship, respect, and fair play has remained a constant, forming the bedrock of modern tennis etiquette.

Importance of Tennis Etiquette in Modern-Day Tennis

In the hustle and bustle of modern-day tennis, with its high-stakes tournaments and intense competition, you could question the significance of etiquette. However, the importance of these conventions cannot be overstated. Tennis etiquette is vital in maintaining the spirit of the game and ensuring it remains enjoyable for everyone involved.

Tennis etiquette helps ensure fair play by discouraging actions that could give an unfair advantage or disrupt the opponent's play. For instance, players are expected to call their shots honestly in non-umpired matches and not intentionally distract their opponent during play.

Moreover, tennis etiquette fosters mutual respect and camaraderie among players. It encourages players to treat their opponents with dignity, regardless of the match's outcome. The customary handshake at the end of the match and the expectation that players will not celebrate excessively after scoring a point is part of this.

In this era where every action is scrutinized and broadcast live worldwide, adherence to tennis etiquette reflects on a player's character and reputation. Players who consistently demonstrate good sportsmanship and respect for the game are often held in high esteem, even if they do not always emerge victorious on the court.

Tennis etiquette, with its emphasis on sportsmanship, respect, and fair play, is integral to the sport. It upholds the integrity of the game and contributes to a positive and enjoyable experience for all involved.

Proper Behavior on the Court

The tennis court is a stage where not only physical prowess and tactical acumen are on display but also a player's character and grace under pressure. The unwritten rules governing a player's conduct on the court reflect the sport's commitment to fair play, respect, and sportsmanship. These guidelines include:

- Respecting the opponent's space by avoiding crossing onto their side of the court.

- Acknowledging if a mistake has been made in calling a ball in or out.

- Not intentionally distracting an opponent during a point.

- Waiting until a point is over to challenge a call.

- Not excessively celebrating a point or a win.

- Shaking hands with the opponent and the umpire at the end of a match.

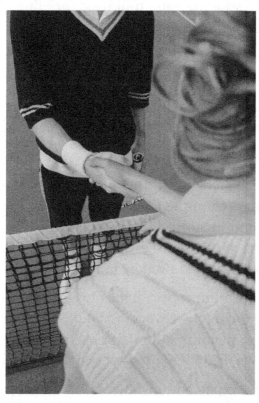

20. You must shake hands with your opponent and the umpire at the end of a match. Source: https://www.pexels.com/photo/woman-in-black-long-sleeve-shirt-and-white-pants-5739231/

Examples of Improper Behavior on the Court

Despite the well-understood guidelines for behavior, instances of improper conduct surface occasionally, providing lessons on what not to do on a tennis court. Examples of bad behavior include:

- Audibly cursing or shouting in frustration, disrupting the game's flow, and potentially distracting the opponent.

- Smashing or throwing a racket in anger can be dangerous and is a sign of poor sportsmanship.

- Questioning an umpire's or line judge's call aggressively or disrespectfully.

- Celebrating excessively after winning a point, especially if it taunts or disrespects the opponent.

- Refusing to shake hands with the opponent or umpire after a match is a clear sign of disrespect.

The Effects of Improper Behavior on the Court

Improper behavior on the court has various negative effects. It can disrupt the game's flow, distract, or intimidate opponents, and create a hostile or unpleasant atmosphere. Bad behavior tarnishes the sport's image, particularly in professional matches viewed by millions worldwide.

Additionally, improper behavior can incur penalties according to the tennis governing bodies' rules. For example, players can be penalized points or entire games for repeated code violations, including unsportsmanlike conduct.

Moreover, repeated instances of improper behavior damage a player's reputation within the tennis community and among fans. It usually leads to a loss of respect from peers, reduced fan support, and affects sponsorship opportunities.

Respect for Opponents and Officials in Tennis

The essence of tennis etiquette and sportsmanship lies in respect – respect for the game, respect for self, and, importantly, respect for opponents and officials. A tennis match is not merely a competition against an adversary but a shared experience between two athletes striving for excellence. Similarly, officials play a crucial role in ensuring fair play and deserving of recognition and respect.

Respecting opponents is acknowledging their skills, accepting their fair victory, and being gracious in defeat. It means avoiding actions unfairly interrupting their play or causing unnecessary distress.

Respecting officials is understanding their role in maintaining the game's fairness and accepting their decisions without argument, even when they seem unfavorable. It means treating them with courtesy and refraining from questioning their integrity.

Examples of Disrespectful Behavior Toward Opponents and Officials

Despite the clear expectations for respect, there are unfortunate instances when these principles are not adhered to. Examples of disrespectful behavior toward opponents and officials include:

- Berating or mocking an opponent during a match.
- Making dishonest line calls in non-umpired matches.
- Refusing to shake hands with an opponent after a match.

- Arguing aggressively with officials over their decisions.

- Making derogatory remarks or gestures toward officials.

The Effects of Disrespectful Behavior Toward Opponents and Officials

Disrespectful behavior toward opponents and officials significantly tarnishes the spirit of the game. It creates a hostile environment, increasing tension and potential conflict on the court. Disrespectful behavior disrupts the game flow and distracts players and officials from their primary focus.

Like improper behavior, disrespectful conduct can result in penalties, ranging from point deductions to disqualification, depending on the offense's severity. Tennis governing bodies have strict rules against unsportsmanlike conduct, and disrespect toward opponents or officials falls under this category.

Moreover, repeated instances of disrespectful behavior can harm a player's reputation. It can lead to a loss of respect among peers and fans, negatively affect a player's standing in the tennis community, and impact career prospects.

Dealing with Challenges and Disputes

Like any competitive sport, tennis is not without its share of challenges and disputes. These can range from disagreements over line calls, especially in non-umpired matches, to conflicts about perceived unsportsmanlike behavior. Other common disputes involve the rule's interpretation, perceived distractions caused by an opponent, or disagreements with officials' decisions.

How to Handle Challenges and Disputes in Tennis

The principles of fair play and sportsmanship should always guide the handling of challenges and disputes in tennis. Here are some general guidelines:

1. In the case of disagreement over line calls, the benefit of the doubt should go to the opponent. In umpired matches, players can request an official review if available.

2. Disputes over rules should be resolved by referring to the official rulebook. The umpire has the final say in interpreting and enforcing the rules in official matches.

3. If a player feels intentionally distracted by their opponent, they should address the issue respectfully, directly with the opponent, or via an official.

4. Disagreements with an official's decision should be handled in the correct manner. While players have the right to request clarification or lodge a formal protest, they should accept the official's decision as final.

The Importance of Good Sportsmanship in Resolving Challenges and Disputes

Good sportsmanship is the glue that holds the fabric of tennis etiquette together, especially in resolving challenges and disputes. It allows players to navigate the inevitable ups and downs of a match with dignity and respect, fostering a positive atmosphere even in disagreements.

Good sportsmanship encourages players to be honest and fair, although it could cost them a point or a match. It discourages gamesmanship and unethical behavior to gain an unfair advantage.

Moreover, good sportsmanship helps maintain the sport's integrity. It sends a message to spectators, especially young and impressionable fans that tennis is a game where character matters as much as skill and strategy.

Inspiring Examples of Tennis Etiquette and Sportsmanship

Tennis history is replete with athletes who have demonstrated impressive skills on the court and remarkable sportsmanship. These players have left a lasting legacy not only with their game but also with their conduct.

One notable example is Arthur Ashe, a champion on and off the court. Known for his grace, humility, and dignity, Ashe was a paragon of sportsmanship throughout his tennis career. His respectful demeanor toward opponents and officials set a high standard for those who followed.

Billie Jean King, another noteworthy figure, redefined sportsmanship by advocating for equality in tennis. Her fight for equal prize money and respect for female athletes transcended the court's bounds, demonstrating the power of sportsmanship in driving social change.

More recent examples include players like Roger Federer and Rafael Nadal, who have given the world some of the greatest tennis matches in history. Their rivalry is characterized by intense competition and, more importantly, mutual respect and admiration. Their conduct on the court, marked by courtesy, respect for officials, and graciousness in victory or defeat, is a testament to their sportsmanship.

The Impact of Good Sportsmanship on the Tennis Community

The impact of good sportsmanship on the tennis community is profound and multifaceted. By demonstrating respect for opponents, officials, and the game, players who exemplify good sportsmanship set a positive example for others to follow.

These examples of sportsmanship encourage a culture of respect and fair play within the tennis community. They set the tone for how players, from professionals to amateurs, should conduct themselves on the court. They also foster a supportive and respectful environment, making the sport more enjoyable for everyone.

Moreover, good sportsmanship significantly shapes the public perception of tennis. Players who demonstrate high sportsmanship enhance the sport's image, making it more attractive to fans, sponsors, and future athletes.

Furthermore, these examples of sportsmanship are a powerful reminder that tennis is not only about winning matches and tournaments. It's about character, respect, and mutual understanding. These lessons extend beyond the court and can influence the attitudes and behaviors of players in their broader lives.

Exemplars of tennis etiquette and sportsmanship provide a blueprint for engaging with the sport respectfully and dignifiedly. Their impact on the tennis community is profound, promoting a culture of respect and fair play, enhancing the sport's image, and teaching valuable life lessons.

Chapter 8: Scoring and Match Play

Understanding scoring in tennis is pivotal to playing and appreciating the game. As a unique system, it determines winners and losers and adds a layer of strategic depth to match play, influencing players' decision-making and tactics.

The scoring system in tennis includes points, games, sets, and matches, each escalating in value and importance. This hierarchy of scores significantly influences the rhythm of the game. Points build into games, games build into sets, and sets accumulate to decide the outcome of the match.

The system's unique structure, including its love-deuce-advantage terminology and winning by two clear points or games in certain situations, adds a distinctive flavor to tennis. It also introduces an element of suspense, as the advantage can swing rapidly between players, keeping spectators on the edge of their seats.

Moreover, the scoring system affects players' strategies and mental resilience. Every point matters and can change the momentum of a game, set, or match. As a result, players must maintain extreme focus and adaptability, showcasing the sport's mental and physical demands.

Understanding Scoring and Tiebreakers

The scoring system in tennis starts at the point level. A player earns points in each game, with the first point won labeled as '15', the second '30', and the third '40'. If a player wins the next point at '40', they generally win the game, unless the score is tied at '40,' which is 'deuce.' To win the game, a player must win two consecutive points from deuce. The first point won from deuce is an 'advantage.'

Multiple games make up a set. To win a set, a player must win at least six games and be ahead by two games. If the game score in a set reaches 6-6, a tiebreaker is typically played to determine the set winner.

A match consists of an odd number of sets, usually best-of-three or best-of-five. The player who wins the majority of the sets wins the match.

Importance of Winning Games and Sets

Each point won brings a player closer to winning a game, each game won brings them closer to winning a set, and each set won brings them closer to winning the match. Therefore, winning games and sets is crucial in tennis, as it directly influences the match outcome.

Moreover, accumulating game and set wins impacts a player's strategy and their opponent's. A lead can allow a player to play more confidently and take more risks, while a deficit might pressure them to change their game plan.

Tiebreakers

A tiebreaker is a specific game played when the score in a set is tied at 6-6. It determines the winner of the set without requiring a two-game lead, which prolongs the set significantly.

Tiebreakers have a unique scoring system. Instead of the traditional 15-30-40-game scoring, points in a tiebreaker are counted using ordinary numbers. The first player to reach at least seven points and lead by two points wins the tiebreaker and the set. If the score reaches 6-6 in the tiebreaker, play continues until one player leads by two points.

The server in a tiebreaker changes after the first point and then every two points after that. Players also switch ends of the court every six points to account for potential advantages or disadvantages caused by wind, sun, or other external conditions.

Playing Singles Matches

Importance of Fitness and Footwork in Singles Matches

Fitness and footwork form the backbone of a successful singles tennis match. Physical fitness enables a player to maintain high energy throughout the match, ensuring optimal performance from the first serve to the last point. Stamina, strength, speed, and agility are essential fitness components for tennis.

On the other hand, footwork is about precision and mobility. Good footwork allows players to reach the ball in time and position themselves optimally for each shot. Proper footwork improves balance, timing, and power, leading to more accurate and effective shots.

Serving Tips for Singles Matches

The serve is a critical shot in singles play. A strong, accurate serve can give the server an immediate advantage in the point. Here are some serving tips for singles matches:

1. **Variety:** Mix up serve speeds, spins, and directions to keep the opponent guessing.

2. **Placement**: Aim for the corners of the service box to stretch the opponent and open up the court for the next shot.

3. **Second Serve**: A reliable second serve is crucial in avoiding double faults. It's often wise to prioritize accuracy and consistency over power for the second serve.

Groundstroke Strategies for Singles Matches

Groundstrokes are the most common shots in tennis and form the basis of many rallies. Here are some strategies for utilizing groundstrokes effectively in singles matches:

1. **Depth:** Deep groundstrokes can push the opponent back, making it harder for them to attack.

2. **Angles:** Angled shots can pull the opponent wide, opening up space in the court.

3. **Shot Selection:** Choosing the right shot for each situation is crucial. For instance, a powerful forehand might be appropriate for an attack, while a high, looping shot is better for defense.

Mental Toughness and Focus on Singles Matches

Mental toughness and focus are as important as physical skills in singles tennis. Players must maintain concentration throughout the match, manage their emotions under pressure, and stay positive when things aren't going well. Mental toughness helps a player stay in the match during tough times and seize opportunities when they arise.

Playing Doubles Matches

Communication between Partners in Doubles Matches

21. Partners must communicate during doubles matches. Source: Gastón Cuello, CC BY-SA 4.0 <https://creativecommons.org/licenses/by-sa/4.0>, via Wikimedia Commons: https://commons.wikimedia.org/wiki/File:YOGBA_2018_-_Tennis_-_Women%27s_Doubles_Final_15.jpg

Effective communication between partners is key to coordinating movements, strategizing shots, and maintaining morale in doubles matches. Partners should communicate before and after points to plan and adjust strategies, identify opponents' weaknesses, and encourage each other. Non-verbal cues, like hand signals, are essential, especially for serving and net play strategies.

Positioning on the Court in Doubles Matches

Positioning in doubles differs from singles, as it involves two players on each side of the net. The two most common formations are the standard formation (partners on the same service line) and the Australian formation (partners on opposite service lines). The choice between these formations depends on the situation and the team's strategy.

Typically, when a team serves, one player serves, and the other stands near the net to cut off volleys and pressure the opponents. When returning the serve, one player usually stays back to handle deep returns, while the other stays near the net or mid-court, depending on the strategy.

Serving Strategies for Doubles Matches

Serving in doubles matches involves more strategy than singles due to two opponents and a partner on the court. Here are some strategies for doubles serving:

1. **Placement:** Serving down the middle limits the angles for the return and sets up the net player for a volley. Serving out wide can stretch the opponents and potentially open up the court.

2. **Teamwork:** The net player should be ready to intercept returns, especially when the server serves wide or down the middle.

3. **Variety:** Mixing up serves keeps the opponents guessing and prevents them from getting into a rhythm.

Net Play and Volleying in Doubles Matches

Net play is crucial in doubles matches. Teams that control the net often control the point, as volleys and smashes at the net can end points quickly. Here are some tips for net play and volleying:

1. **Anticipation:** A good net player anticipates the direction of the return and positions themselves to volley.

2. **Volley Technique**: Effective volleys in doubles are usually firm and angled away from opponents. Low volleys toward the opponents' feet are also effective.

3. **Communication:** Partners must communicate well to avoid going for the same shot and cover the court effectively.

Tennis Tactics for Different Court Surfaces

Tennis is played on various court surfaces, each with distinct characteristics influencing the ball's speed, bounce, and player movement. These surfaces include clay, grass, and hard court.

1. **Clay Courts:** These courts, often red or green, are made from crushed shale, stone, or brick. Clay surfaces slow down the ball and produce a high bounce, leading to longer rallies.

2. **Grass Courts**: Grass courts provide the fastest game of tennis, with the ball often skidding low off the surface. The bounce on grass courts is often unpredictable, adding an additional challenge.

3. **Hard Courts:** These courts vary in speed but are generally faster than clay and slower than grass. The bounce on hard courts is high and relatively predictable, making them suitable for several playing styles.

Adjusting Tactics for Different Court Surfaces

The playing surface significantly influences how a match unfolds. Therefore, players must often adjust their tactics according to the court surface.

1. **Clay Courts**: Patience and endurance are vital on clay, as points typically last longer. Topspin-heavy shots are often effective, as the high bounce can challenge the opponent. Defensive skills are also highly valuable due to the slower game speed.

2. **Grass Courts:** On grass, aggressive serve-and-volley play is effective due to the low bounce and fast speed. Flat and slice shots that stay low can be troublesome for opponents. Quick reactions and good volleying skills are typically advantageous on this surface.

3. **Hard Courts:** Hard court matches often favor well-rounded players due to the surface's balanced nature. Baseline and net play are viable strategies, and versatile shot selection is often beneficial.

Tips for Playing on Clay, Grass, and Hard Court

When playing on different surfaces, players should consider the following tips:

1. **Clay Courts:**

   • Improve slide control for better movement.

- Develop a consistent, high-bouncing topspin to push opponents back.

- Practice patience and plan for longer rallies.

2. Grass Courts:

- Work on serving accuracy and speed. A powerful, well-placed serve can gain an immediate advantage.

- Hone volley skills. Quick, low volleys can be particularly effective.

- Develop a reliable slice shot to keep the ball low and challenge opponents.

3. Hard Courts:

- Enhance overall fitness. The predictable bounce and medium pace often lead to extended rallies, demanding good endurance.

- Work on shot versatility, as power and finesse shots are effective.

- Practice baseline play and net approaches, as the hard courts' balanced nature allows varied strategies.

Understanding the characteristics of different tennis court surfaces and adjusting tactics accordingly is critical to competitive play. Players can maximize their chances of success by tailoring their strategies to each surface.

Chapter 9: Tips and Tricks for Beginners

Like learning a new skill, beginning tennis can be a challenging yet exciting endeavor. As beginners navigate their way through the basics of tennis, they will undoubtedly encounter various challenges. Understanding fundamental techniques, learning the rules, and developing a feel for the game take time and practice.

However, this initial learning curve should not be a deterrent. Instead, it's an opportunity to build a solid foundation for future improvement. This chapter provides tips and tricks useful as shortcuts or guides, offering beginners effective ways to grasp essential concepts, avoid common mistakes, and improve their game more efficiently.

The importance of learning tips and tricks for beginners cannot be overstated. They provide insight gained from experienced players and coaches, saving beginners from trial and error, often accompanied by learning a new sport. These tips and tricks cover a wide range of topics, from technique and strategy to equipment and fitness.

In essence, these pieces of advice are valuable resources that can expedite the learning process, help beginners improve faster, and make their initial tennis experience more enjoyable and rewarding.

Common Mistakes and How to Avoid Them

Beginner tennis players often face many challenges as they navigate the game. Some challenges stem from common mistakes that, while entirely natural as part of the learning process, can hinder progress if not addressed. Understanding these common errors and how to avoid them can significantly enhance the learning curve for beginners.

1. **Gripping the Racquet Too Tightly:** Many beginners grip the racquet too tight, leading to less control over shots and could cause arm discomfort. A firm but relaxed grip allows better racquet control and flexibility.

2. **Incorrect Footwork:** Beginners often overlook the importance of proper footwork. Standing flat-footed or failing to move the feet can result in awkward shots and a lack of balance.

3. **Hitting Too Hard:** Many novice players believe power is the key to winning points. As a result, they often hit the ball too hard, leading to a lack of control and more unforced errors.

22. Hitting the ball too hard can result in incorrect shots. Source: https://commons.wikimedia.org/wiki/File:YOGBA_2018_-_Tennis_-_Women%27s_Doubles_Final_15.jpg

4. **Neglecting the Serve:** The serve is one of the most important shots in tennis, yet beginners often don't give it the attention it deserves. Poor serving technique can put a player at a disadvantage right from the start of a point.

5. **Failing to Use Topspin:** Flat shots might seem simpler at first, but neglecting to learn topspin can limit a player's shot options and control, especially as they progress.

Tips on How to Avoid These Mistakes

1. **Relax the Grip:** To avoid gripping the racquet too tight, beginners should learn to maintain a firm but relaxed grip. This balance allows better shot control and prevents arm discomfort.

2. **Improve Footwork:** To address footwork issues, beginners can practice constantly moving their

feet during play, even when not hitting the ball. Drills focusing on lateral, forward, and backward movement and quick directional changes are beneficial.

3. **Focus on Control, Not Power:** Beginners should focus on controlling and placing the ball accurately rather than hitting it as hard as possible. As control improves, they can gradually add more power to their shots.

4. **Practice the Serve**: Beginners should dedicate a portion of each practice session to serve drills. Working with a coach or experienced player will correct technique issues and develop a reliable, effective serve.

5. **Learn to Use Topspin**: Beginners should learn to incorporate topspin into their shots early on. Topspin enhances shot control, increases the margin for error by pulling the ball down into the court, and eventually becomes a weapon as the player's skills progress.

Mistakes are a natural part of the learning process; understanding the common mistakes made by beginners in tennis and knowing how to avoid them significantly smoothens the learning journey. With patience, practice, and mindful correction of these errors, beginners can improve their game more efficiently and enjoyably.

Remember, regardless of their current expertise, every successful player started as a beginner and made mistakes. Here are a few examples of successful tennis players who overcame initial obstacles and mistakes to reach the pinnacle of the sport:

1. **Novak Djokovic:** Early in his career, Djokovic struggled with fitness and had a reputation for retiring from matches due to heat and breathing difficulties. However, he addressed these issues by significantly changing his diet and fitness regimen, which marked improvements in his endurance and overall performance. Today, Djokovic is known for his exceptional fitness and resilience on the court.

2. **Rafael Nadal**: Known for his impressive topspin, Nadal had to adapt his game to use this technique effectively. He started playing tennis with a two-handed forehand and backhand. Understanding the limitations of this style, especially on grass surfaces, he worked hard to develop an effective one-handed topspin forehand, which has become one of his greatest weapons.

3. **Serena Williams:** Serena's aggressive playing style often caused unforced errors early in her career. However, she worked tirelessly to balance her power with control, leading to a more consistent yet still powerful game. Serena's serve, now considered one of the best in women's tennis, also took years of practice to perfect.

4. **Roger Federer:** In his early years, Federer was known for his fiery temper and would often lose focus during matches, causing unnecessary errors. Recognizing this, he worked on his mental game and learned to stay calm and composed under pressure. This mental strength has become one of Federer's biggest assets in his illustrious career.

These examples demonstrate that even the greatest tennis players have had to overcome mistakes and challenges. Their success is a testament to their perseverance, practice, and willingness to learn and adapt. Beginners can rectify their mistakes and continually improve their game.

Practicing Effectively

Tennis is a complex sport requiring combined physical skills and strategic understanding. Regular practice and consistency are crucial to developing these abilities. Practice allows beginners to hone their techniques and build muscle memory, making movements more automatic over time. In addition, consistent practice helps improve fitness, coordination, and mental toughness, which are critical components of a successful tennis game.

The Importance of Practice and Consistency in Tennis

Consistency in practice is key in tennis. Regular, focused practice sessions allow beginners to work on their techniques, correct mistakes, and gradually improve their skills. Additionally, consistency in hitting the ball - aiming for depth and accuracy rather than strength - can be a game-changer for beginners, as it puts pressure on the opponent and reduces unforced errors.

Drills and Training Techniques for Beginners

Beginners can use several effective drills and training techniques to improve their tennis skills:

1. **Mini Tennis Drill:** This drill requires players to stand close to the net and rally to keep the ball in the service boxes. It helps improve control and touch and is a great way to warm up.

2. **Baseline Drill:** Two players rally from the baseline, aiming to keep the ball within the singles court. This drill helps improve groundstrokes and consistency.

3. **Serve and Return Drill**: One player serves while the other returns. This drill allows both players to practice their serves and returns in a match-like situation.

4. **Figure 8 Drill:** This footwork drill involves moving in a figure 8 pattern around two cones or marks on the ground. It helps improve agility and movement on the court.

5. **Wall Hitting:** Hitting a ball against a wall helps improve shot accuracy, consistency, and reaction time. It's also a great way to practice when a playing partner is unavailable.

Tips on How to Improve Form and Footwork through Practice

Improving form and footwork is a crucial aspect of tennis enhanced through targeted practice. Here are some tips:

1. **Work on Balance:** Maintaining balance while hitting shots is essential. Drills involving hitting while on the move improve balance.

2. **Use the Correct Grip**: The correct grip for different shots (e.g., Eastern grip for forehands, Continental grip for serves and volleys) can significantly improve a player's form.

3. **Focus on Follow-Through:** A full follow-through ensures shots are hit with proper spin and direction.

---

4. **Keep Feet Moving**: Staying light on the feet and constantly moving them enhances a player's ability to reach the ball and maintain balance.

5. **Shadow Swing:** Practicing swings without a ball can help players focus on their form and footwork.

Effective practice is a vital component of success in tennis. By focusing on consistency, engaging in targeted drills, and working on form and footwork, beginners can significantly enhance their skills and enjoyment of the game.

Mental Preparation and Focus on the Court

Tennis is often described as a mental game. While physical skills and technique are undeniably important, the ability to concentrate, stay composed under pressure, and make strategic decisions in the heat of a match is equally as crucial. Therefore, mental preparation is an integral aspect of tennis that beginners should not overlook.

Mental preparation in tennis includes several components. Entering each match with a clear strategy, understanding the opponent's strengths and weaknesses, and adapting the strategy as the match unfolds are all equally important. It also helps a player manage emotions and stress, maintain focus and concentration, and display resilience during setbacks.

In essence, mental preparation sets the stage for optimal performance. It enables players to tap into their full potential by ensuring their mind is focused, resilient, and ready to face the challenges of the match.

Techniques for Improving Focus and Concentration on the Court

Improving focus and concentration in tennis is often a matter of practice, like improving physical skills. Here are several techniques to help:

1. **Mindfulness:** Being fully present in the moment, focusing on the task at hand, and not getting distracted by external factors or internal thoughts. Regular mindfulness meditation can help train the mind to focus better during matches.

23. Meditating regularly can help you focus better during matches.
Source:
https://unsplash.com/photos/rOn57CBgyMo?utm_source=unsplas
h&utm_medium=referral&utm_content=creditShareLink

2. **Mental Imagery:** Also known as visualization, this technique involves imagining various match situations and the appropriate responses. It helps prepare the mind for different scenarios and improves decision-making during matches.

3. **Routines:** A set routine or ritual before serving or returning serve helps players focus and block out distractions.

4. **Breathing Exercises:** Deep, controlled breathing can calm the mind, reduce anxiety, and improve focus.

5. **Goal Setting:** Setting specific, measurable, achievable, relevant, and time-bound (SMART) goals for each practice session or match gives players clear focus and improves concentration.

Tips for Staying Calm and Composed During Matches

Staying calm and composed during tennis matches significantly enhances performance. Here are some tips to achieve this state of mind:

1. **Embrace Pressure:** Players should learn to embrace pressure instead of viewing it as negative. Pressure is inherent in the game, and effectively managing it leads to better performance.

2. **Control the Controllable:** Players should focus on aspects of the game they can control, such as their preparation, effort, and reactions, rather than external factors like the weather or the opponent's actions.

3. **Positive Self-Talk:** Encouraging yourself during a match, especially during challenging moments, helps maintain a positive mindset and stay composed.

4. **Take a Break:** Between points, players should use the time to relax, regroup, and refocus. This

break can help lower stress and maintain composure.

5. **Learn from Mistakes:** Instead of getting frustrated by mistakes, players should view them as learning opportunities. This perspective can reduce stress and improve resilience.

Mental preparation and focus are critical aspects of tennis. Tennis players can enhance their performance on the court by applying techniques to improve focus and concentration and adopting strategies to stay calm and composed. The mind is a powerful tool in the game of tennis.

Overcoming Challenges and Building Confidence

Like any sport, tennis has challenges and obstacles, from mastering the sport's technical aspects and dealing with physical limitations or injuries to overcoming mental pressures and performance anxieties. Yet, it is through facing and overcoming these challenges that a player can truly grow. Furthermore, significantly navigating these obstacles contributes to building confidence and self-belief on the court.

Dealing with Challenges and Obstacles in Tennis

Challenges in tennis can be technical, physical, and mental. Technical challenges entail mastering the sport's techniques, such as serving, volleying, or perfecting backhand and forehand shots. Physical challenges might involve dealing with injuries, increasing stamina, or improving agility and speed. Mental challenges include handling pressure, maintaining focus, and staying resilient in defeat.

To overcome these challenges, a player must adopt a growth mindset, viewing obstacles not as insurmountable problems but as opportunities for learning and improvement. Regular and focused practice and constructive feedback from a coach or mentor can help overcome technical difficulties. Physical challenges necessitate a balanced approach, including suitable training, adequate rest, nutrition, and injury management. Often, addressing mental challenges requires adopting techniques such as mindfulness, mental imagery, and positive self-talk and gaining experience through match play.

Tips for Building Confidence and Self-Belief on the Court

Building confidence and self-belief in tennis is a gradual process from within. Here are some tips for fostering these qualities:

1. **Celebrate Progress**: Recognizing and celebrating improvements, however small, can boost confidence. Acknowledging progress and appreciating the effort is important.

2. **Set Realistic Goals:** Setting achievable goals for each practice session or match provides a sense of purpose and enhances motivation and confidence when those goals are met.

3. **Visualize Success**: Visualization or mental imagery of successful shots or match wins fosters a positive mindset and increases self-belief.

4. **Embrace Challenges**: Viewing challenges as opportunities to learn and grow, rather than threats, builds resilience and confidence.

5. **Positive Self-Talk**: Encouraging yourself with positive affirmations and motivational thoughts enhances self-belief.

Examples of Successful Players Who Overcame Challenges in Their Careers

Many successful tennis players have faced and overcome significant challenges in their careers, which have strengthened their resolve and confidence.

1. **Andre Agassi**: Early in his career, Agassi was known more for his flamboyant style than his tennis. He faced numerous criticisms and struggled with self-belief. However, he overcame these challenges, changed his approach to the game, and became one of the most successful and respected players in tennis history.

2. **Monica Seles**: After being the victim of an on-court attack, Seles faced severe physical and emotional trauma. Despite this, she made a successful comeback to the sport, demonstrating remarkable resilience and mental strength.

3. **Stan Wawrinka:** Wawrinka spent many years in the shadow of his more successful Swiss compatriot, Roger Federer. However, he didn't let this deter him. He worked hard on his game and mental strength, eventually breaking through to win multiple Grand Slam titles.

Chapter 10: Analyzing Games of Top Players and Their Secret Strategies

Tennis is a game of strategy, technique, mental fortitude, and physical prowess. By studying top players' games, beginner players gain valuable insight into the strategies and techniques that have led to their success. Each player brings a unique approach to the game, and understanding these nuances can provide a wealth of knowledge and inspiration for aspiring tennis players.

Before delving into the analysis of top players' games and their strategies, here is an inspirational story of a legendary tennis player who climbed the ranks from a rookie to a world champion.

Rafael Nadal, the renowned Spanish tennis player. Born in Manacor, a small town on the island of Mallorca, Spain, Nadal started playing tennis at the incredibly young age of three under the guidance of his uncle, Toni Nadal.

His journey wasn't always smooth. Nadal faced numerous hurdles, including significant physical challenges. Early in his career, he suffered from a congenital foot problem, leading to frequent injuries and, at one point, could have ended his career. However, Nadal's tenacity and determination saw him through. He adapted his playing style to manage the injuries and continued to grow as a player.

24. *Rafael Nadal is known for his powerful playing style. Source: Yann Caradec, CC BY-SA 2.0 <https://creativecommons.org/licenses/by-sa/2.0>, via Wikimedia Commons: https://commons.wikimedia.org/wiki/File:Rafael_Nadal_Roland_Garros_2012.jpg*

Nadal, known as the "King of Clay," has a powerful and aggressive playing style, characterized by his heavy topspin groundstrokes, quick footwork, and tenacious court coverage. He is especially known for his unprecedented success on clay courts, but his adaptability and versatility have seen him triumph on all surfaces.

His mental toughness, resilience, and never-give-up attitude are as much a part of his success as his physical skills and technique. Nadal's career is a testament to the power of perseverance, hard work, and a deep love for the sport.

From his humble beginnings in Manacor to his rise as a multiple Grand Slam champion, Rafael Nadal's journey is an inspiring example of how determination, hard work, and passion can become an extraordinary success.

The next sections delve into the games of top players, uncovering the strategies and techniques that have propelled them to the pinnacle of tennis.

The Importance of Studying the Techniques of Top Players

The techniques of top tennis players often represent the pinnacle of what is currently achievable in the sport. They reflect the players' physical skills, understanding of the game, strategies, and adaptation to different opponents and situations. By studying these techniques, you can learn the mechanics of different strokes, the strategic use of the court, the importance of footwork, and the game's mental aspects.

A detailed understanding of these techniques provides a source of inspiration. It can motivate players to improve their game and set new personal goals. Moreover, it can provide a benchmark against which players can measure their progress.

1. **Roger Federer**: Federer is known for his effortless style and flawless technique. His serve is one of his biggest weapons, characterized by its precision, variety, and unpredictability. Federer often uses his serve to set up advantageous positions in the rally, aiming for the corners of the service box to stretch his opponents. His forehand

is another powerful tool, with its heavy topspin and ability to hit winners from almost any position on the court. Federer's one-handed backhand, though less powerful, is highly versatile, enabling him to hit slicing defensive shots and aggressive topspin shots. His footwork is also a key aspect of his game, allowing him to position himself optimally for every shot.

2. **Rafael Nadal**: Nadal's game is characterized by his incredible physicality, relentless intensity, and masterful topspin. His forehand, whipped with heavy topspin, is a major weapon, enabling him to push opponents back and create opportunities to hit winners. Nadal's two-handed backhand is solid and reliable, capable of high-topspin defensive shots and flat, aggressive shots. His serve has evolved from a high-spin, high-percentage shot to a more powerful and varied stroke. Nadal's footwork and speed are exceptional, enabling him to cover the court effectively and run down almost any ball.

3. **Novak Djokovic**: Djokovic's game is built around his extraordinary defensive skills, flexibility, and precision. His two-handed backhand is widely regarded as one of the best in the game, characterized by his power, consistency, and ability to hit precise angles. Djokovic's forehand is also formidable, capable of high-topspin defensive shots and flat, powerful winners. His serve is accurate and reliable, often used to set up a strong first strike in the rally. Djokovic's footwork and court coverage are among the best in the game,

allowing him to defend against powerful hitters and turn defense into offense.

Examples of How These Techniques Have Contributed to Their Success

The techniques used by Federer, Nadal, and Djokovic have been instrumental in their success. Federer's precise serving and versatile groundstrokes have allowed him to dictate play and keep opponents on their back foot. His footwork enables him to move around the court easily and fluidly, positioning himself optimally for each shot.

Nadal's heavy topspin forehand and relentless intensity have enabled him to dominate on clay and excel on all other surfaces. His footwork and speed allow him to cover the court effectively, making him one of the toughest players to hit winners against.

Djokovic's defensive skills and precision have made him a formidable opponent on all surfaces. His ability to maintain consistency and precision under pressure, coupled with his flexibility and court coverage, allow him to outlast opponents in long rallies and turn defense into offense.

Studying the techniques of top tennis players provides invaluable insight into the game's strategies, skills, and mental aspects. The examples of Federer, Nadal, and Djokovic illustrate how diverse and varied these techniques can be, reflecting each player's unique strengths and styles. Aspiring players can enhance their understanding of the game and improve their performance on the court by analyzing and learning from these techniques.

Identifying Key Strategies and Tactics Used by Professionals

Raw skill and physical prowess alone do not guarantee success in tennis. The importance of strategy and tactics cannot be overstated. These cognitive aspects of the game often distinguish a good player from a great one.

A tennis strategy is a player's overall plan to gain an advantage over their opponent. This plan is based on a player's understanding of their strengths and weaknesses and of their opponent. A well-thought-out strategy can direct a player's efforts more efficiently, enabling them to exploit their opponent's weaknesses while maximizing their strengths.

Tactics are the specific actions or sequences of actions players implement in their strategy. For example, a player may have a strategy of keeping their opponent on the move to exploit a perceived lack of fitness. The tactics to implement this strategy might include several cross-court shots, drop shots followed by lobs, and frequent changes of pace and spin.

Strategies and tactics in tennis are multifaceted and include elements like shot selection, court positioning, variations in spin and speed, psychological maneuvers, and adaptations to different court surfaces and playing conditions.

1. **Serena Williams:** Serena Williams is renowned for her powerful and aggressive playing style, which she uses to dominate opponents and dictate the match pace. One of her key tactics is her potent serve, arguably one of the best in the history of women's tennis. She uses her serve to score aces and set up short returns she can attack with her

powerful groundstrokes. Additionally, Williams is known for her ability to hit powerful and accurate shots while on the run, allowing her to turn defensive situations into offensive ones. Her shot selection is often powerful baseline play mixed with unexpected drop shots, keeping her opponents constantly on edge. Despite her aggressive style, Williams can also display remarkable patience, waiting for the perfect moment to unleash her powerful shots.

2. **Martina Navratilova**: Navratilova's game was built around her exceptional net play and her ability to effectively execute serve-and-volley tactics, a strategy not as commonly seen in today's baseline-dominated game. By rushing to the net after her serve, she put immediate pressure on her opponents, forcing them to hit accurate passing shots or lobs. Navratilova also excelled at doubles play, which helped her develop outstanding court awareness and sharp reflexes, particularly around the net. Her ability to anticipate her opponent's shots and cut-off angles at the net were key elements of her tactical approach. Despite her aggressive net play, she also had a solid baseline game, with powerful and accurate groundstrokes, providing a strong foundation for her attacks.

3. **Steffi Graf**: Graf, known for her powerful forehand and footwork, used her speed and agility to dictate the game's pace. Her forehand, often referred to as the "Fraulein Forehand," was a major weapon in her arsenal, which she used to hit powerful, flat shots, keeping her opponents on the defensive. Graf had a versatile and effective

tactical approach, coupled with her slice backhand, which she used to change the pace of the ball and disrupt her opponents' rhythm. Graf's serve was significant in her strategy. She had a powerful and accurate serve that she often followed to the net, particularly on grass courts. Her footwork and speed allowed her to effectively cover the court and maintain an aggressive position, forcing her opponents into errors.

Examples of How These Strategies Have Contributed to Their Success

1. **Serena Williams**: Williams' powerful serve and aggressive playing style have been central to her success. Her serve allows her to control points from the outset, while her powerful groundstrokes and ability to hit winners from defensive positions enable her to dictate play and keep her opponents on the back foot. These tactics have contributed to her remarkable record, including 23 Grand Slam singles titles.

2. **Martina Navratilova**: Navratilova's serve-and-volley tactics and exceptional net play were key to her dominance, particularly on grass courts. Her aggressive approach and keen court sense put constant pressure on her opponents, forcing them to make difficult shots. Her strategies led to an extraordinary career, including 18 Grand Slam singles titles and a record 31 Grand Slam women's doubles titles.

3. **Steffi Graf:** Graf's powerful forehand, slice backhand, and effective serve-and-volley tactics allowed her to dominate women's tennis in her

era. Her aggressive, all-court playstyle and exceptional footwork and fitness secured her 22 Grand Slam singles titles.

By understanding and analyzing the strategies and tactics of these legendary tennis players, players gain valuable insight into the different playing styles and strategic approaches successful in tennis. Each of these champions had a unique approach to the game, demonstrating the many paths to success in the sport.

Applying Insights from Top Players to Improve Your Game

Gleaning insights from the techniques and strategies of top tennis players cultivates a deeper understanding of the game and valuable lessons to improve your performance on the tennis court.

Observing and analyzing the playing styles of tennis champions such as Roger Federer, Serena Williams, and Rafael Nadal offers a wealth of knowledge. From understanding how they adapt their tactics based on the opponent to learning about their workout routines and mental preparation, these insights are priceless for aspiring players.

1. **Understanding Strategies**: Players should study professionals' strategies during different phases of the game and understand how these tactics change based on the situation and the opponent. For example, you may observe how Federer uses his serve to set up points or how Nadal uses his heavy topspin forehand to push opponents back and create opportunities.

2. **Analyzing Techniques:** The technical aspects of top players' games, such as stroke mechanics,

footwork, and body positioning, provide invaluable lessons. Slow-motion videos can be particularly helpful for understanding these techniques. For instance, studying Serena Williams' powerful serve or Steffi Graf's forehand provides insights into how these players generate power and control.

3. **Emulating Mental Toughness:** The mental aspect of tennis is as important as physical skill and technique. Watching champions handle pressure and maintain focus helps players enhance their mental toughness. Djokovic's ability to stay calm under pressure and to turn the tide in crucial moments of the match is a case in point.

How to Implement These Strategies and Techniques in Your Game

1. **Focus on Fundamentals**: Before trying to emulate advanced strategies and techniques, it's crucial to have a strong foundation in tennis basics, including sound stroke mechanics, footwork, and an understanding of the game's rules and strategies.

2. **Start Small:** When implementing a new strategy or technique, start small and gradually increase complexity. For example, if working on improving your serve like Serena Williams, begin by focusing on one aspect at a time, like the toss, the swing, or the follow-through.

3. **Practice Consistently:** Consistent practice is key to integrating new techniques and strategies into your game. It includes physical practice on the court and mental rehearsal and visualization.

4. **Seek Feedback:** Working with a coach or a more experienced player who can provide feedback and guidance is often helpful. They can identify weaknesses, suggest adjustments, and provide drills to practice new techniques or strategies.

5. **Be Patient and Persistent**: Improving at tennis takes time and persistence. Don't be discouraged by initial difficulties or setbacks. Remember, even top professionals have faced challenges and have worked hard to develop their skills and strategies.

How Players Have Successfully Applied These Insights to Improve Their Game

Players at all levels have successfully applied insights from top professionals to improve their game. For instance, many club players have improved their serve by studying the techniques of players like Roger Federer or Serena Williams and incorporating elements of their serving style into their game.

Junior players have also benefited from studying professional strategies. For example, they might watch how Rafael Nadal constructs points and uses his heavy topspin to create high-bouncing balls, making it difficult for his opponent to attack. By emulating this strategy, they can make their game more robust and versatile.

Recreational players have found success by applying professional techniques. Something as simple as improving footwork, a fundamental aspect of the game often overlooked at amateur level, can lead to significant improvements. Watching how professionals like Novak Djokovic or Steffi Graf move on the court gives valuable insight into efficient court coverage and positioning.

Ultimately, studying and applying insights from top tennis players can significantly improve a player's game. It provides a roadmap for success, offering techniques to emulate, strategies to implement, and an inspiration source for continuous improvement.

Chapter 11: Winning Strategies and Improving Performance

With its blend of physical, mental, and strategic elements, tennis offers a compelling journey of self-improvement, discipline, and relentless pursuit of mastery. Whether it's the thrill of hitting a perfect cross-court winner, the satisfaction of outsmarting an opponent, or the resilience built from battling through a five-set match, tennis provides countless opportunities to grow as a player and as an individual.

Becoming a winner in tennis is not necessarily about standing on the podium or being crowned a champion. Rather, it's about striving for personal excellence, pushing beyond perceived limitations, and constantly seeking to improve performance on and off the court. It's about understanding the game deeply, honing your skills diligently, and stepping onto the court, match after match, with the unwavering determination to play your best.

Developing a Winning Mindset and Confidence

The role of mindset and confidence in tennis cannot be overstated. Like a player's physical ability and technical skills are integral to success in tennis, so is their mental strength. The difference between a good and a great player, or a tight match won and lost, often lies in the mind's domain.

A winning mindset in tennis is characterized by focus, resilience, belief, and an unyielding desire to improve. This mindset allows players to stay calm under pressure, maintain concentration during lengthy matches, and bounce back from setbacks with renewed determination.

25. Believing you can win will help you maintain focus. Source: https://unsplash.com/photos/_XTY6lD8jgM?utm_source=unsplash&utm_medium=referral&utm_content=creditShareLink

Focus is crucial for executing techniques and strategies effectively. It involves paying attention to the task, whether hitting a serve, returning a difficult shot, or implementing a game plan. Without focus, it's easy for a player to become distracted or make unforced errors.

Resilience is recovering quickly from difficulties and adapting to challenging situations. It could mean coming back from a set down, adjusting tactics when the initial game plan isn't working, or dealing with unfavorable conditions like a hostile crowd or challenging weather.

Belief in their abilities gives players the confidence to take risks, like going for a difficult shot or sticking to an aggressive game plan. Players who believe in themselves are likelier to play to their full potential and less likely to be deterred by temporary setbacks.

An unyielding desire to improve drives players to refine their skills continually, seek out new strategies, and push their limits. This desire to improve and to never be complacent is a hallmark of a winning mindset.

Confidence, closely related to belief, is another critical factor in tennis success. A confident player steps onto the court believing they can win, regardless of the opponent or circumstances. Confidence enhances performance by reducing nerves, encouraging positive risk-taking, and promoting a positive attitude.

However, confidence should not be mistaken for arrogance. It's about accurately assessing your abilities and believing in your capabilities to perform well, not underestimating the opponent or neglecting preparation. It's a delicate balance requiring self-awareness and humility.

Developing a winning mindset and confidence in tennis is a continuous process, often cultivated through experiences, good and bad, on and off the court. It involves mental training, self-reflection, and a deep commitment to personal growth. The next sections give more insight into developing these critical mental components, setting the foundation for winning strategies and improving performance.

Techniques for Developing a Winning Mindset and Boosting Confidence

Cultivating a winning mindset and confidence in tennis is as vital as honing physical skills. Here are some strategies to help foster these critical mental attributes:

1. **Setting Clear Goals**: Establishing Specific, Measurable, Achievable, Relevant, and Time-bound (SMART) goals guides a player's journey. It could be about mastering a new stroke, improving fitness, or winning a certain number of matches. Achieving these goals can significantly boost a player's confidence and provide progress and direction.

2. **Mental Visualization:** This technique envisions success on the tennis court, such as executing a perfect serve or winning a crucial point. By mentally rehearsing these scenarios, players can enhance their confidence and prepare their minds for the actual game situation.

3. **Positive Self-Talk:** A player's internal dialogue with themselves can significantly influence their mindset and confidence. Encouraging self-talk reinforces belief in a player's skills, while negative self-talk is detrimental to performance. Players should consciously practice positive self-talk, turning every internal interaction into a motivation and confidence source.

4. **Embrace Challenges**: Challenges and setbacks are inherent in every tennis player's journey. Players foster resilience and a positive attitude

toward personal development by adopting a growth mindset and viewing these challenges as opportunities for learning and improvement.

5. **Regular Mindfulness Practice:** Mindfulness, or the practice of being fully present and engaged in the moment, helps players improve focus and reduce anxiety. Techniques like meditation or focused breathing exercises should be incorporated into a player's routine to enhance mindful awareness.

6. **Physical Fitness and Preparation**: A player's physical condition plays a significant role in their confidence. Regular fitness training, proper nutrition, and adequate rest ensure a player feels physically prepared and confident when stepping onto the court.

7. **Seek Constructive Feedback:** Regular feedback from coaches, trainers, or fellow players will identify areas for improvement and reinforce progress. This feedback is a valuable tool for boosting confidence and ensuring continuous improvement.

8. **Celebrate Success:** Recognizing and celebrating successes, no matter how small, reinforces positive feelings and boosts confidence. Whether mastering a new stroke or winning a tough match, acknowledging these victories significantly impacts a player's self-belief and motivation.

The tennis world is full of players showing how a winning mindset can propel careers and create legends. Here are a few examples of players who've developed a winning mindset and its impact on their careers.

1. **Steffi Graf:** Graf's career was characterized by exceptional focus and mental toughness. Her ability to stay calm in high-pressure situations and her relentless pursuit of success were key contributors to her 22 Grand Slam singles titles.

2. **Bjorn Borg**: Known for his cool and composed demeanor on the court, Borg's mental strength was instrumental in his success. Even in adversity, his ability to maintain his composure showcased his winning mindset and led to 11 Grand Slam singles titles.

3. **Kim Clijsters**: Clijsters' resilience and never-give-up attitude were evident when she made a successful comeback after becoming a mother, a testament to her mental toughness. Her ability to juggle family responsibilities with the demands of professional tennis demonstrated her strong mindset.

4. **Pete Sampras:** Sampras' mental toughness was a defining feature of his game. Known for his capability to elevate his performance under pressure, Sampras' unshakeable belief in his abilities contributed to his 14 Grand Slam singles titles.

5. **Justine Henin**: Despite her relatively smaller stature than her competitors, Henin's mental strength and determination were immense. Her belief in her abilities, coupled with her tactical intelligence, allowed her to overcome bigger and stronger opponents, leading to seven Grand Slam singles titles.

These players offer compelling examples of how cultivating a winning mindset can lead to extraordinary achievements in tennis. Their careers underline the importance of mental strength and self-belief in reaching the pinnacle of this sport.

Analyzing and Exploiting Your Opponent's Weaknesses

Analyzing and exploiting your opponent's weaknesses is a critical aspect of competitive tennis and any sport. Understanding the areas where your opponent struggles gives you a strategic edge and significantly enhances your chances of emerging victorious.

The importance of understanding your opponent's weaknesses is crucial. This understanding allows you to formulate a game plan targeting these vulnerabilities, increasing the chances of your opponent making errors. For example, if your opponent has a weak backhand, make a conscious effort to direct your shots to that side, forcing them to rely on their weaker stroke. Similarly, if your opponent often cracks under pressure, use this knowledge to up the intensity at crucial moments to elicit mistakes or provoke weaker serve returns.

Analyzing your opponent's weaknesses involves careful observation and study. You can employ several strategies to achieve this. For instance, watch previous matches or observe them during the warm-up. Listening to coaches' or teammates' insights who have played against them can also be useful. Additionally, paying close attention to your opponent's body language and responses under various pressures can reveal valuable information about their mental and physical game. How do they react to different playing styles? Do they show signs of frustration or defeat when they're trailing in a match?

Once you've identified your opponent's weaknesses, the next step is to exploit them. Devise a game plan to challenge these weak areas continually. However, it's crucial to remain adaptable as your opponent could adjust their tactics to compensate for their weaknesses.

While focusing on your opponent's weaknesses is a key strategy, playing to your strengths is equally important. Your gameplay should strike a balance between pressuring your opponent's weak points and maximizing your strong points. If you're known for your powerful serve, for instance, don't neglect this advantage in your pursuit of exploiting your opponent's weaknesses.

Techniques for Identifying and Exploiting Your Opponent's Weaknesses

1. **Observing Previous Matches:** Analyzing your opponent's games gives insight into their gameplay, strengths, and weaknesses. Look for recurring patterns or habits you can exploit.

2. **Analyzing During Warm-Up:** Use the warm-up period to assess your opponent's skills. Pay attention to their serving, returns, and forehand and backhand strokes. Any apparent weaknesses could be potential targets during the match.

3. **Studying Body Language**: A player's body language reveals a lot about their confidence and mental state. Signs of frustration or nervousness could indicate mental weaknesses you can take advantage of.

4. **Consulting with Coaches or Teammates**: If your coaches or teammates have previous experience with your opponent, their insight could be valuable in identifying weaknesses.

5. **Adapting During the Match:** Be ready to adjust your strategy based on your opponent's performance during the match. If you spot a previously unnoticed weakness, don't hesitate to exploit it.

Examples

1. **Rod Laver:** Known for his versatility and tactical acumen, Laver was adept at identifying and exploiting his opponent's weaknesses. His ability to play excellently from all areas of the court put constant pressure on his opponent's weak points.

2. **Billie Jean King**: King was known for her tactical intelligence. She had a keen ability to read her opponent's game and target their vulnerabilities, which was significant in her winning 12 Grand Slam singles titles.

3. **Boris Becker:** Becker's aggressive serve-and-volley game often put his opponents on the back foot. He was particularly effective at exploiting opponents who were weak on the return or uncomfortable at the net.

Implementing Winning Strategies in Practice and Matches

Achieving success in tennis hinges on developing winning strategies and effectively implementing these strategies in practice and matches. Here are some tips to help you put your strategies into action successfully:

1. **Practice with Purpose**: Every practice session should have a purpose aligned with your strategy. If your strategy involves improving your serve, focus on that during your practice sessions. Use drills to improve your accuracy, speed, and placement. Remember, the practice aims to strengthen your strengths and transform your weaknesses into strengths.

2. **Simulate Match Conditions:** Recreate match conditions during your practice sessions as much as possible. For instance, practice under the same weather conditions, on the same surface, or time of day as your upcoming match. The more you can make your practice mirror your match, the better prepared you'll be to implement your strategies when it counts.

3. **Use Visualization Techniques:** Visualization is a powerful tool for implementing winning strategies. Imagine executing your strategy perfectly during a match. Visualize your movements, shots, and emotions. It will help you mentally prepare for the match and increase confidence in your strategy.

4. **Develop a Game Plan:** Before every match, develop a detailed game plan based on what you know about your opponent and your game. This plan should outline the strategies you intend to use, like targeting your opponent's backhand or drawing them to the net with short slices. A clear plan can help you stay focused and make effective strategic decisions during the match.

5. **Be Adaptable:** A plan is important, but it's equally important to adapt it based on what's happening during the match. If your strategy isn't working, don't be afraid to change it. The best players can adjust their tactics in response to their opponent's game and the match's evolving dynamics.

6. **Learn from Each Match:** After each match, reflect on what went well and what didn't. Did you implement your strategy effectively? What could you have done differently? Use these understandings to inform future strategies and implementation.

Implementing winning strategies in practice and matches requires thoughtful planning, focused practice, adaptability, and continuous learning. You can enhance your ability to put your strategies into action effectively and increase your chances of success on the tennis court by applying these tips consistently.

Chapter 12: Professional Practice Drills for Skill Development

In tennis's fast-paced, demanding, and competitive world, skill development is not just an option—it's a necessity. Mastering the fundamental skills of tennis, from perfecting your serve to honing your forehand and backhand, is crucial to elevating your gameplay and achieving success on the court.

As the old saying goes, practice makes perfect. In tennis, practice is critical. Through rigorous, consistent, and purposeful practice, players can refine their skills, eliminate weaknesses, and enhance their strengths.

26. Practice drills will help you refine your techniques. Source:
https://www.pexels.com/photo/girl-playing-tennis-8224683/

While casual practice or playing matches certainly helps improve your game, incorporating professional practice drills into your training routine offers additional advantages. These drills help you master the technical aspects of tennis and improve fitness, agility, speed, and mental toughness which are all essential components of a well-rounded tennis player.

Top-ranked players around the world, like Roger Federer and Serena Williams, use professional practice drills to fine-tune their skills and prepare for high-stakes matches. However, these drills are not reserved solely for professionals. Players at all levels can benefit from these exercises by adapting them to their skill and training goals.

This chapter explores various professional practice drills to help you develop your skills and take your tennis game to new heights. Whether a beginner looking to learn the basics, an intermediate player aiming to eliminate your weaknesses, or an advanced player seeking to refine your skills, these drills offer valuable guidance and inspiration.

Embrace these professional practice drills' challenges. Incorporate them into your training routine, push your limits, and watch as your skills, confidence, and performance on the court improve. Remember, every champion was once a contender who refused to give up. The journey to tennis mastery begins with the decision to pick up the racket and the commitment to practice, practice, and practice some more.

The symbiosis between tennis and practice is fundamental. Each stroke in tennis, whether a power-packed serve, a delicate drop shot, or a cross-court forehand, is a composite of numerous technical elements. The correct footwork, the right grip, the precise timing, the optimal swing path—each component must be executed correctly for the stroke's success. This precision is achieved and sustained only through practice.

Moreover, tennis is a sport where strategy and mental toughness are pivotal. It's not enough to merely have good strokes; you must know when to use them, how to construct points, exploit an opponent's weaknesses, and manage the ebb and flow of momentum during a match. Therefore, strategic acumen and mental resilience are honed through repetitive practice and match-play scenarios.

The Benefits of Practicing Consistently

Consistency in practice is key to progress in tennis. It facilitates a deeper understanding of the game and allows the development of strong, reliable tennis skills. One benefit of consistent practice is developing muscle memory. Each time you practice a stroke, neural pathways are created in your brain. The more you practice, the stronger these pathways become, enabling you to execute the stroke more accurately and reliably over time.

Consistent practice fosters resilience. Tennis is a game of adversities—unforced errors, difficult opponents, unfavorable match situations, and mental and physical fatigue. Regularly practicing teaches you to overcome these adversities and develop the mental toughness to stay focused, composed, and confident, regardless of the circumstances.

The Role of Practice in Developing and Improving Skills

Through targeted and strategic practice, players can work on specific aspects of their game that need improvement. For example, you can focus on serve drills to improve your power, accuracy, and consistency if your serve is a weak spot. If your net game needs work, practice volleys, and overheads until they become a strength rather than a weakness.

Furthermore, the practice provides a safe space for experimentation. You can try new techniques, strategies, or adjustments to your strokes without the pressure of a competitive match situation. This freedom to experiment and adjust is crucial for skill development and improvement.

Tennis practice is a multifaceted tool. It is a means to hone technical skills and a vehicle for strategic learning, mental strengthening, and overall player development. Through the rigors and rewards of practice, tennis players evolve, improving their game and understanding and love of the sport.

Exploring Practice Drills Used by Professional Players

The path professional tennis players tread is of relentless practice and skill refinement. Their training routines are packed with numerous practice drills, each targeting specific aspects of their game. The next section explores key practice drills professionals use, analyzes their benefits, and looks at examples of players who have incorporated these drills into their training regimes.

Overview of Commonly Used Practice Drills by Professional Players

1. **Serve Practice Drills:** The serve, the only shot in tennis a player has complete control over, is often a focal point in professional practice sessions. Drills vary from aiming at targets to practicing second serves under pressure.

2. **Return of Serve Drills:** Returning a serve effectively is as crucial as the serve. Professionals often spend significant time practicing returning serves from different angles and speeds.

3. **Groundstroke Drills:** These drills focus on improving consistency, accuracy, and power of forehand and backhand shots. They often involve hitting balls to specific areas of the court.

4. **Volley Drills**: Since net play can often be a deciding factor in matches, volley and overhead drills are integral to professional training.

5. **Footwork Drills:** Good footwork is the foundation of effective tennis play. Drills focusing on agility, speed, and efficient court movement are common in professional training routines.

6. **Endurance and Sprint Drills**: Tennis is as much a physical endurance test as it is a skills test. Professionals incorporate intense fitness drills, including long-distance running for endurance and sprints for explosive speed, into their routines.

Analysis of Each Drill and Its Benefits

1. **Serve Practice Drills:** These drills improve the power, spin, and placement of serves. They enhance a player's ability to serve effectively under pressure. For instance, a drill could involve aiming serves at targets placed in different service boxes, mimicking the variety of serves required in a match.

2. **Return of Serve Drills:** These drills enhance a player's ability to react quickly, judge the ball's trajectory, and return serves with precision. They help a player neutralize a powerful serve or turn a return into an offensive shot.

3. **Groundstroke Drills:** Drills like the 'down the line' and 'cross-court' improve shot precision, consistency, and power. They help players practice constructing points, controlling the play's pace, and dictating rallies.

4. **Volley Drills:** These drills improve a player's quick transition to the net, sharpen their volleying skills, and enhance their overhead smash. They help players become more versatile, enabling them to switch from baseline rallies to net play easily.

5. **Footwork Drills**: These drills enhance a player's agility, speed, and balance on the court. Improved footwork leads to better shot execution, as players can position themselves optimally for each stroke.

6. **Endurance and Sprint Drills:** These drills enhance a player's fitness, allowing them to maintain high performance throughout a match. Improved endurance and speed give a player a significant edge, especially in long, grueling matches.

Examples:

Serve Practice Drills

John Isner: His huge serve has been a pivotal part of his game, so he undoubtedly places emphasis on serving drills and techniques to consistently hit aces.

Return of Serve Drills

Andy Murray: His ability to return even the biggest serves has been key to his success, so he has likely spent significant time perfecting his return techniques.

Groundstroke Drills

Caroline Wozniacki: Her counter-punching style relies on consistent and accurate groundstrokes, so she likely does many repetitive drills for her forehand and backhand.

Volley Drills

Kevin Anderson: At 6 feet 8 inches tall, volleying can be challenging for Anderson. He likely focuses heavily on volley drills to improve his net game.

Footwork Drills

Simona Halep: Her diminutive stature requires excellent movement and court coverage. Footwork and agility drills are surely an important part of Halep's training.

Implementing Effective Practice Techniques for Skill Development

The road to tennis mastery is paved with effective practice. It's where skills are sharpened, strategies are tested, and a player's mettle is forged. However, not all practice is equal. Effective practice techniques, implemented with consistency and dedication, can significantly accelerate skill development and performance improvement. This section covers the best practices for implementing effective practice techniques, structuring your routine for maximum skill development, and the importance of consistency and dedication.

Best Practices for Implementing Effective Practice Techniques

1. **Set Specific Goals:** Each practice session should have a clear, specific goal. Whether improving serve accuracy, refining volley technique, or enhancing footwork, defining your objective helps maintain focus and provides a benchmark for progress.

2. **Quality Over Quantity:** It's not about how long you practice but how well. Concentrate on your practice's quality. Ensure each stroke is executed with proper technique and each drill is performed with full intensity. Mindless repetition can reinforce bad habits while mindful practice helps develop good ones.

3. **Use Drills That Simulate Match Conditions: Practice** should mimic the conditions you'll face in matches. Use drills simulating actual game scenarios. This drill will improve your skills and

make you more comfortable and adaptable during matches.

4. **Seek Feedback**: Whether from a coach, a training partner, or a video analysis, feedback is crucial. It gives an outside perspective on your performance, highlighting areas for improvement you might overlook.

5. **Rest and Recover:** Effective practice requires proper rest and recovery. Overtraining can lead to fatigue, injury, and burnout. Ensure you have adequate rest days in your training schedule, and incorporate recovery techniques like stretching, massage, and good nutrition.

How to Structure Your Practice Routine for Maximum Skill Development

1. **Warm-Up and Cool-Down:** Every practice session should begin with a thorough warm-up to prepare your body for the intense activity ahead and end with a cool-down period to help your body recover.

2. **Skill-Specific Drills:** Dedicate time blocks to drills targeting specific skills to improve. For example, start with simple serve placement drills before moving on to more complex serve-and-volley drills if you're focusing on serving.

3. **Match Play**: Include some match play in your practice sessions. It allows you to apply the skills and strategies you've been working on in a game setting.

4. **Fitness Training:** Don't neglect physical fitness. Incorporate strength training, endurance

exercises, and flexibility drills into your routine. A fit player is less likely to get injured and likelier to maintain good form and intensity throughout a match.

5. **Mental Training**: Tennis is as much a mental game as a physical one. Spend time on mental training, such as visualization exercises, mindfulness training, or learning to handle pressure and manage emotions during a match.

The Importance of Consistency and Dedication in Implementing Practice Techniques

Consistency and dedication are the heart and soul of effective practice. Without consistency, improvements will be slow and hard to come by. Each practice session builds upon the last, reinforcing the neural pathways associated with specific movements and strategies. Consistent practice helps solidify these pathways, leading to more reliable, automatic execution of skills.

Dedication fuels the effort and determination to persist in challenges and setbacks. It's the driving force that gets you on the court day after day, pushing your limits, refining your skills, and striving to be the best player you can be.

Remember, there are no shortcuts to tennis mastery. It's a journey of countless steps, each taken with purpose, consistency, and unwavering dedication. Embrace the process, relish the challenges, and let your love for the game fuel your quest for improvement. As the legendary tennis player Arthur Ashe once said, "Start where you are. Use what you have. Do what you can." With effective practice techniques and a committed mindset, you can unlock your full potential on the tennis court.

Advanced Practice Drills for Skill Development

Advanced practice drills are an essential tool for tennis players, taking their skills to the next level. These drills push players beyond their comfort zones, challenging them to refine their technique, improve decision-making, and enhance physical fitness. The drills described below require a high level of skill and concentration and are regularly used by top-level players to keep their game sharp and competitive.

1. **The Nadal Drill**

   - **Description**: The Nadal Drill, named after the 20-time Grand Slam winner Rafael Nadal, is an intense groundstroke drill focusing on consistency, placement, and stamina. The drill starts with the player at the center baseline. The coach or training partner feeds the ball alternately to the player's forehand and backhand, forcing the player to run laterally across the court to hit each shot. The Nadal Drill is a baseline drill focusing on improving the forehand and backhand shots.

   - **Benefits:** This drill improves a player's groundstroke consistency and accuracy under pressure. It enhances lateral movement and endurance, as the player must move quickly from side to side while maintaining high intensity throughout the drill.

2. **Serve + 1 Drill**

   - **Description**: The Serve + 1 Drill improves a player's control of the point from the serve. The drill involves the player serving and immediately playing out the next shot, regardless of the return. The goal is to win the point within the first two shots - the serve and the subsequent aggressive groundstroke.

- **Benefits:** This drill helps players develop an aggressive mindset, encouraging them to seize the initiative from the start of the point. The Serve + 1 Drill enhances serve accuracy and power, first-strike groundstrokes, and quick transition from serving to rallying.

3. **The In-and-Out Drill**

- **Description:** The In-and-Out Drill is a comprehensive drill to improve all-court play. The drill begins with the player hitting three groundstrokes from the baseline, moving forward to the net to hit three volleys, and moving back to the baseline to hit three more groundstrokes. The drill is repeated several times without stopping.

- **Benefits**: This drill effectively enhances a player's transition between baseline and net play. It improves groundstroke power and accuracy, volleying skills, footwork, and court positioning. Players can become more comfortable and effective in all areas of the court by practicing this drill.

4. **The Down-The-Line Drill**

- **Description:** The Down-The-Line Drill enhances a player's control and precision. The player and the coach or training partner rally exclusively down the line in this drill, aiming to keep every shot as close to the line as possible without hitting it out.

- **Benefits:** This drill improves shot accuracy and control, as hitting down the line requires more precision than hitting cross-court. It helps players develop their ability to change the ball's direction, a key skill in match play to outmaneuver opponents.

5. The Suicide Drill

- **Description:** The Suicide Drill is a rigorous fitness drill that improves shot execution under fatigue. The player starts at one corner of the baseline, sprints to the net, touches it, and then sprints back to the opposite corner of the baseline before sprinting to the net again. The coach or training partner feeds the player balls they must hit on the run.

- **Benefits:** This drill significantly boosts a player's fitness, speed, and endurance. It improves shot execution under physical stress, a crucial skill in long, grueling matches. Furthermore, it enhances a player's footwork and agility, as they have to quickly change direction while maintaining speed and balance.

6. The Approach Shot Drill

- **Description:** The Approach Shot Drill is tailored to improve a player's ability to effectively transition from the baseline to the net. The player starts at the baseline, and the coach or partner feeds a short ball. The player hits an approach shot and follows it to the net to play out the point with volleys or overheads.

- **Benefits:** This drill aids in enhancing the quality of approach shots, which can determine net points' success. It boosts a player's volley and overhead skills under pressure. Moreover, it improves decision-making regarding when to approach the net and the shot to play.

7. The Cross-Court Drill

- **Description:** The Cross-Court Drill improves a player's consistency and accuracy on cross-court shots. The player and coach or partner rally cross-court, keeping the ball within a coned-off area. The aim is to maintain a continuous rally for as long as possible.

- **Benefits**: This drill helps players develop consistency and accuracy on cross-court shots, which are fundamental in match play. It improves shot depth control, as the coned-off area encourages players to hit their shots deep to keep their opponents on the defensive.

8. The Overhead Smash Drill

- **Description:** The Overhead Smash Drill is a specialized drill to improve a player's ability to hit effective overhead smashes. The player starts at the net, and the coach or partner feeds high lobs. The player must hit an overhead smash for each lob.

- **Benefits:** This drill enhances a player's overhead smash technique and accuracy, an essential skill for finishing points at the net. It improves a player's ability to judge and position themselves correctly for high balls.

9. The Side-to-Side Drill

- **Description:** In the Side-to-Side Drill, the player begins at the center of the baseline, and the coach or partner feeds balls alternately to each **corner, forcing the player to move laterally and hit on the run.**

- **Benefits:** This drill improves a player's lateral movement and footwork, essential for covering the court effectively. It enhances a player's ability to hit accurate shots while on the move, a key skill in today's fast-paced game.

10. The Drop Shot and Lob Drill

- **Description**: In the Drop Shot and Lob Drill, the player starts at the baseline, and the coach or partner feeds a short ball. The player must hit a drop shot, followed by a lob over the coach or partner who attempts to close the net.

- **Benefits:** This drill enhances a player's touch and feel on delicate shots like the drop shot and lob. It improves a player's adaptation to different situations and uses various shots to outwit the opponent.

When incorporated into a regular training regimen, each drill can help tennis players hone their skills and become more adaptable during match play. Remember, while drills can significantly improve a player's game, they require consistent practice and dedication to be truly effective.

Conclusion

The voyage of this book has been a comprehensive exploration of tennis. It started at the absolute basics and culminated with advanced strategies and techniques.

The guide commenced with a thorough understanding of the rules and regulations governing the tennis game. The intricacies of the tennis racket - its components, its function, and the impact of different materials, sizes, and strings on a player's performance - were explored in depth. The essence of tennis etiquette, an integral part of the sport that often gets overlooked, was also emphasized.

The guide transitioned into the game's physical aspects. Various basic and advanced techniques were dissected meticulously, from the serve - the single most important shot in tennis - to groundstrokes, volleys, and specialty shots. Scoring, a unique aspect of tennis that is often confusing for beginners, was demystified.

Strategies for singles and doubles play were discussed, emphasizing the importance of teamwork in doubles and the role of tactics in the outcome of a tennis match. The guide addressed the physical and mental aspects of tennis, highlighting the importance of fitness, agility, and mental toughness in a sport demanding as much from the mind as it does the body.

Lastly, advanced practice drills were included to help aspiring players take their skills to the next level. These drills, used by top-level players, refine technique, improve decision-making, and enhance physical fitness.

This guide provided a complete understanding of tennis, from fundamental concepts to advanced skills and strategies. The journey of learning tennis is a rewarding one, filled with challenges, improvements, and, most importantly, fun. As with anything, the key to mastery is persistence and practice. Even the greatest players in the world started as beginners. So, with dedication, passion, and proper guidance, anyone can embrace the sport and experience the joy of playing tennis.

This guide was meant for you, an aspiring tennis player. Please leave a review to encourage other keen beginner tennis players to learn as much as you did.

References

Collinson L, Hughes M. Surface effect on the strategy of elite female tennis players. J Sports Sci 2003;21:266–7.

Ferrauti A, Pluim BM, Busch T, et al. Blood glucose responses and incidence of hypoglycaemia in elite tennis under practice and tournament conditions. J Sci Med Sport 2003;6:28–39.

Hohm J. Tennis technique tactics training: play to win the Czech way. Toronto: Sport Books Publisher, 1987:18.

McCarthy PR, Thorpe RD, Williams C. Body fluid loss during competitive tennis match-play. In:Lees A, Maynard I, Hughes M, Reilly T, editors.Science and racket sports, 2nd edition. London: E & FN Spon, 1998:52–55.8'

O'Donoghue P, Ingram B. A notational analysis of elite tennis strategy. J Sports Sci 2001;19:107–15.

O'Donoghue P, Liddle D. A notational analysis of time factors of elite men's and ladies' single tennis on clay and grass surfaces. In:Lees A, Maynard I, Hughes M, Reilly T, editors.Science and racket sports, 2nd edition. London: E & FN Spon, 1998:241–246.

Smekal G, Von Duvillard SP, Rihacek C, et al. A physiological profile of tennis match play. Med Sci Sports Exerc 2001;33:999–1005.

Struder HK, Hollmann W, Duperly J, et al. Amino acid metabolism in tennis and its possible influence on the neuroendocrine system. Br J Sports Med 1995;29:28–30.

Therminarias A, Dansou P, Chirpaz M-F, et al. Cramps, heat stroke and abnormal biological responses during a strenuous tennis match. In:Reilly T,Hughes M, Lees A, editors.Science and racket sports, 1st edition. London: E & FN Spon, 1994:28–31